The SHADOW *of*
BABEL

WOODY D. WILSON

Published by
CrossHouse Publishing
PO Box 461592
Garland, Texas 75046-1592
Copyright Woody Wilson 2009
All Rights Reserved
Printed in the United States of America
by Lightning Source, LaVergne, TN
Cover design by Dennis Davidson
Photography by Nathan Wilson
Except where otherwise indicated, all Scripture taken from the
NEW AMERICAN STANDARD BIBLE,
Copyright 1960, 1962, 1963, 1968, 1971, 1972, 1975, 1977,
by the Lockman Foundation. Used by permission.
ISBN 978-1-934749-40-1
Library of Congress Control Number: 2008943174

TO ORDER ADDITIONAL COPIES FOR $15.95 EACH (ADD $3.00
SHIPPING FOR FIRST BOOK, $.50 FOR EACH ADDITIONAL BOOK)
CONTACT
CROSSHOUSE PUBLISHING
PO BOX 461592
GARLAND, TEXAS 75046-1592
www.crosshousepublishing.com
877-212-0933 (toll free)

What others are saying ...

"*The Shadow of Babel* grapples with the important, the lasting and the eternal. It challenges and inspires. Woody Wilson's experience as a communicator, missionary, and pastor well qualifies him to speak to the topic of sharing the gospel. You will enjoy his stories and the life-changing principles. Read this book, put into practice the lessons learned, and let God use you in His great work!"

Dr. Doug Munton, Author, Warriors in Hiding
Senior pastor, First Baptist Church, O'Fallon, IL

"Wilson has written a book to inspire all believers to arise and share the hope that is within them. Having served on the mission field, he used his training to bring focus to one of the most critical issues facing the Church today and provides authentic solutions for every believer toward participation in what I call the meat and potatoes of evangelism—relational evangelism. May everyone who reads this book be inspired to share his or her faith in Christ with another and experience the heavenly joy of being used by God to affect someone's life for eternity as a minister of reconciliation."

Rick Ballard, Executive Director
Collin Baptist Association

"Warning! The reading of Woody Wilson's book will dust the cobwebs off of your witness and might just make you uncomfortable. I dare you to read it anyway. Read it to retune your testimony. Read it to stretch your faith. Read it for the hundreds who will come to Christ as a result."

Robert M. Barge, Revivalist with Wherever Ministries
Author of The Souljourn *and* The Jesus Test

"Whether you consider yourself a gifted evangelist or a believer who simply knows he or she needs to be a better Christian witness, *The Shadow of Babel* will challenge and encourage you. Woody Wilson transforms witnessing from an isolated life compartment that is only entered into upon special occasions into a natural life process. His tips help take the fear out of evangelism and show how our words to non-Christians can be both relevant and effective."

Frank Banfill, President
MaxPoint Ministries

"How can the church clearly communicate the message of the Gospel, which is the most important information a person will ever hear, in this Informational Age in which people are constantly bombarded with millions of bits of information calling for their attention? That is the question that Woody Wilson answers in his book *The Shadow of Babel: Speaking Jesus to a Language-Challenged World*. Through the lens of his experience of learning a foreign language in order to communicate the Gospel cross-culturally, Wilson challenges his readers to "find their voice" in order to clearly communicate the Good News of salvation to this present generation. Contrasting the biblical events of the building of the tower of Babel and the coming of the Holy Spirit at Pentecost in his Introduction, Wilson throughout his book challenges the contemporary church to "step out of the Shadow of Babel" in a confused, language-challenged world and "step into the light of Pentecost" whereby believers individually and corporately communicate their faith in order that this postmodern generation can hear the Gospel in their own language and respond to the claims of Christ. I appreciate the fresh, unique approach to personal evangelism employed by the author and highly recommend this book to any believer desirous of learning to communicate his faith more effectively in our language-challenged world."

Dr. Preston L. Nix
Associate Professor of Evangelism and Evangelistic Preaching
occupying the Roland Q. Leavell Chair of Evangelism
Director of the Leavell Center for Evangelism and Church Health
Chairman of the Pastoral Ministries Division
New Orleans Baptist Theological Seminary

Acknowledgements

I would like to express deep appreciation to the many dedicated spiritual teachers and mentors I have had over the years. The men and women who taught my childhood Sunday School classes instilled in me a genuine love for the Word of God that undergirds my life today. My college and seminary professors nurtured this love and challenged me to base my life and ministry on the unchanging truths of God's self revelation. Two professors at Southwest Baptist University had a profound impact on my life. Gordon Dutile first taught me Greek and inspired me to dig deep into the language of the New Testament. Dan Cochran, professor of philosophy, taught me to think.

During my years at Southwestern Baptist Theological Seminary, I sat at the feet of some great men of God: Curtis Vaughan, Leo Garrett, Roy Fish, Jack MacGorman, T. W. Hunt, William Estep, David Garland, and Justice Anderson to name just a few. I had the privilege of serving as Joel Gregory's grading assistant at a time when he was Southern Baptists' foremost pulpiteer. At Midwestern Baptist Theological Seminary, my doctoral seminars were led by wonderful professors and guest lecturers, such as Gary Smith, Don Whitney, Robin Hadaway, Howard Hendricks, Don Kammerdiener, and Robert Coleman. I am especially indebted to Tom Johnston and Darrell Robinson for their seminar on evangelism. It was during this seminar that I first met Darrell Robinson. He put me in touch with CrossHouse Publishing and graciously wrote the foreword. I am also thankful for those who were kind enough to write an endorsement for this work.

I am thankful for church members across the years who allowed me to train them in evangelism. We have laughed, cried, and prayed together as we have endeavored to tell others about our glorious Savior.

I am so very thankful for my family. My parents raised me with godly fear. My mother was my first Bible teacher and gave me a love of learning; my late father was my friend and pastor and discipled me during my teen-age years. Though his doing so embarrassed me when I was a youth, I cherish the memories of him crying in the pulpit as he passionately preached God's Word. My brothers, Sam and Greg, have helped me become who I am today. Sam and his wife, Barbara, serve the Lord faithfully in their church, as does Greg in his.

My wife is the most beautiful woman in the world. She is a prayer warrior and my biggest fan. Without her my spiritual journey would be incomplete. I am thankful for and proud of our children. Josh and his wife, Jaime, have given us two amazing grandchildren. Josh serves as Youth Pastor at First Baptist Church, Whitewright, Texas. Nathan is using his artistic abilities to chronicle spiritual need around the globe. The photograph on the cover is one he took while on a mission trip to Dublin, Ireland. Matthieu, a student at Southwest Baptist University, serves as Youth Pastor at Olive Point Baptist Church in Preston,

Missouri. Rachel, also a student at SBU, has a beautiful singing voice and a wonderful passion for life.

I am grateful for the encouragement and guidance I have received from Katie Welch at CrossHouse Publishing. She has stepped me through this process with grace and skill. Her enthusiasm is evident in how she goes about her work.

I am especially thankful for the work of Carolyn Wright in proofreading the manuscript and helping me firm up the flow of my thoughts. Her contribution to this book is immense and invaluable.

During my lifetime, I have done many things that bring happiness and a sense of satisfaction and accomplishment. The greatest thing I have ever done, though, is to lead another person to trust Jesus as Lord and Savior. There is no greater joy than this!

TABLE OF CONTENTS

The Shadow of Babel

Foreword

Some things are basic and obvious in the Word of God. First: God loves every single person and desires him or her to be saved. Second: God provided for salvation through the life, death, and resurrection of His only begotten Son, Jesus Christ, who is the one, exclusive way to come to God and be saved. Third: Christ came to "seek and save the lost." Fourth: Every believer is indwelt by Christ Himself and is to join Him in His mission to reach every person with His saving message by personally communicating His Gospel of salvation through his or her personal witness.

In his marvelous and inspiring book, *The Shadow of Babel: Speaking Jesus to a Language-Challenged World*, Dr. Woody Wilson encourages followers of Jesus Christ to open their mouths and personally proclaim the good news of salvation. In his words, "silence is not an option. Not only is our silence a sinful rebellion against God's expressed will, but it threatens to condemn countless millions of souls to a Christless hell."

The reader will enjoy his delightful stories and illustrations. They were gained through his rich experiences as a personal witness, a missionary in the difficult setting of France, and a faithful pastor who equips his members to witness. Dr. Wilson motivates all who read his book to intentionally seek to witness daily by living the Christ-life and by speaking the Words of the Good

News. He not only motivates but shows how every believer CAN DO IT!

The content of this book is totally biblical and is written in excellent and captivating language. It shows the difficulties of communicating understandably in a world of many and diverse languages and cultures (since the Tower of Babel). It shows how to bridge the language and cultural barriers by obeying the principles of Christ. At the end of each chapter are simple, practical helps entitled "INCREASE YOUR WORD POWER."

SILENCE because of fear is the tendency of believers and churches. Dr. Wilson reminds us that the word for "witness" in the New Testament is the Greek word for "martyr." For many early Christians, it was better to die than to stop testifying about Christ. We can and must overcome fear and silence.

The book shows both the positive and the negative power of words. Dr. Woody Wilson has shown in transferrable terms how Christians can share in their own words their personal testimony, present God's plan of salvation, and guide a person through the conversion experience.

EVERY PASTOR, CHURCH, AND BELIEVER WILL PROFIT BY USING THIS BOOK AS A GUIDE TO BE EQUIPPED AND REACH THE LOST FOR CHRIST.

—Darrell W. Robinson, author of *Incredibly Gifted*

Preface

In the midst of writing this book, my wife asked me what inspired me to write it. The inspiration came, quite simply, from a line I had written years before in a missionary newsletter. We were in language school in Tours, France—far away from the familiar, surrounded by those who spoke a language we did not yet understand. The missionary call was daunting. How could we communicate the good news of Jesus when we could not even talk about the weather or order soup in a bistro?

What I wrote in that newsletter was this: "Missions, or cross-cultural evangelism, is lived out in the shadow of Babel and the confusing of the languages, but also in the hope of Pentecost when all the people heard the gospel in their own language." This sentence, which became the thesis of the book, lay dormant in my mind for years until the Holy Spirit brought it back to my consciousness and compelled me to flesh it out in its present form. In that first missionary newsletter, dated July 1987, I went on to write the following:

> As we learn the language of the 55 million people who live in France, we slowly but surely see the hope of communication growing and the frustration of confusion diminishing. We are encouraged, but we still have a very long way to go before we will be fluent. Language study is at the same time fun and frus-

*trating, exciting and exasperating, stimulating and tedious. The
long hours of study are worth it, however, when we are able to
use what we have learned in actual conversation.*

What I wrote back then about learning and using another language may also be instructive as we learn the language of witness. We must move past talking about evangelism and begin to put it into practice in actual conversation.

My wife's question needs to be addressed on a different level, however. Her question seems to inquire: "Why another book on evangelism? Are there not enough books on this subject already?" Again the simple answer is that while there are indeed many excellent books on evangelism, God's people have not yet been convinced that they must speak up for the Lord. Most Christians have never led another person to faith in Jesus. This sad fact was reinforced the other day as I attended an annual gathering of churches in our Baptist association. The Executive Director, wanting to recognize all those who had been involved in mission trips, asked those volunteers to stand. Many across that auditorium did so. Then, wanting to highlight evangelism, he asked all those who had led someone to the Lord to stand. Only a handful stood. I wrote this book because God's people must be motivated to become bold witnesses. Now, I do not believe that this book is the sole answer to this problem, but perhaps it will encourage some—even you! If one person would gain courage from reading these pages and boldly speak Jesus to just one lost person, then I would count it a success. My prayer is that many might do just that!

FINDING OUR VOICE

"Why can dogs understand French, but I can't?" This is a tough question to answer, but then, five-year-olds are known to ask tough questions. We had been on the mission field just long enough to know the frustration of not being able to communicate even the simplest of messages. Worse yet, we did not understand what others were saying to us. In response to my son's question, I tried to explain that the dogs who obeyed French commands were native to France. The French language was their realm of comprehending. Joshua just thought the dogs were very smart.

Communicating Jesus challenges Christians to step out from the shadow of Babel and the confusing of language and into the light of Pentecost when all the people heard the gospel in their own tongue. Genesis 11:1 says, "Now the whole earth used the same language and the same words."[1] The people had one language and a common speech, but they were full of themselves and arrogantly began constructing a monument to their greatness. They built a city and were proceeding with the centerpiece of their kingdom—a great tower reaching to the heavens. Their thoughts must have surely been something like this: "We don't need God. We are building a tower that will make us great. We can find our own way to heaven."

God was not pleased with their building project, however, and "came down to see the city and the tower which the sons of men had built" (Genesis 11:5). Verse 6 tells us that with a common tongue, nothing would be impossible for them to accomplish. This statement alone ought to instruct us that the biggest impediment we have as humans is the lack of communication. The solution to the soaring pride of the people of Babel was to confuse their language. God made it impossible for them to communicate. This was the resolute decision of God. "Come, let us go down and there confuse their language, so that they will not understand one another's speech" (Genesis 11:7). He then scattered them abroad over the face of the earth. The result was that they stopped building the tower.

Over the ages, that nearly completed tower has cast an ominous shadow across humanity. It is a shadow of confusion, misunderstanding, and miscommunication. This shadow extends to all corners of the earth. It is not just a missions problem; it is a dilemma for evangelism as well. Sometimes people who speak the same language mean different things by the words and phrases they use and perceive different meanings from what they hear. To communicate the gospel of Jesus Christ effectively, whether on some distant mission field or across the street, we must step out of the shadow of Babel and into the light of Pentecost.

When the Holy Spirit came upon the believers gathered for prayer in the upper room, a miracle occurred. Scholars debate whether it was a miracle of speech or a miracle of hearing. Regardless, "the crowd came together, and were bewildered because each of them was hearing them speak in his own language" (Acts 2:6). Verse 8 gives their response; "How is it that we each hear them in our own language to which we were born?" Luke, the author of the book of Acts, gives an impressive list of countries and peoples represented there in the streets of Jerusalem. This multinational, multilingual crowd exclaimed with awe, "We hear them in our own tongues speaking of the mighty deeds of God (Acts 2:11).

That day, real communication was established and three thousand souls were saved. The shadow of Babel receded and people understood and responded with faith. Pentecost promises that confusion will not rule the day. Barriers of language and culture, barriers of dialect and accent, barriers of meaning and perception can be powerfully overcome.

God confused the earth's common language to prevent the people from forgetting Him. Now, in thousands of languages and dialects, people seek God and raise their voices to Him in worship. I even believe that God delights in the diversity of it all. On Easter Sunday, 1992, I participated in an amazing display of multiethnic, multilinguistic worship. The worship leader of our small church in the southern suburbs of Paris, France, asked the worshipers to say *Jesus is Lord* in their native tongue. Present that day in our congregation of eighty-eight members and guests were Americans and British who spoke English (although with much different accents and vocabularies), native French speakers, one who spoke Patois (a French/Haitian mix), an Algerian believer who spoke Arabic, and those who spoke four different West African languages. What a beautiful testimony to the power of the gospel! God had gathered together in common faith a people from all over the world. For most of that service, we worshiped in a common language, French. For one glorious moment, however, the air was filled with the sweet melody of a worship that is but a foreshadowing of that day when, in heaven, a great multitude from every nation, tribe, people, and language will stand before the throne and in front of the Lamb and will lift their voices in praise (Revelation 7:9-19).

St. Francis of Assisi is often quoted as saying, "Preach the gospel always. If necessary, use words." He makes a good point. Presenting the gospel is accomplished both by our actions and our words. Sometimes what we do speaks louder than, and therefore nullifies, our words. If we intend to speak the gospel, then we had better be prepared to live it. Some in our world today lean heavily upon acts of charity and ministry, to the exclusion of verbal witnessing. I believe St. Francis himself would agree, if we could ask him, that in our society it is very necessary to use words.

Imagine for a moment a young man who surrendered his life to missions. He was challenged by his pastor to use the gifts that God had given him to proclaim Jesus. He rejoiced that the Lord would choose him and could use his talent. What was that talent, you ask? Why, he was a mime, of course! A very good one at that. He did that "trapped-in-a-box" person very, very well. He walked into a hurricane force wind, leaning heavily against a make-believe gale. He could attract a crowd. When he finished his routine, the audience would always applaud vigorously. There was only one problem—he was a dedicated mime and mimes do not speak. Staying in character, all he had was actions and gestures and, therefore, the result was nothing more than entertainment. Without words, the dramatized actions had little meaning. The process of communication involves "the transmission of a meaningful idea through words and gestures"[2] so that the listener can understand. Gestures without words may not transmit the intended meaning adequately or completely. The goal of communication is to transmit the message in such a way as "to elicit a response from the listener."[3] Hopefully, you get the point. Words—our voices—are necessary if we are to speak Jesus to those around us. Let me add that I have seen a couple of mimes who worked in tandem with a speaking partner. The mime would draw the crowd; the partner would share the gospel. So if you are an aspiring mime, do not throw away your white gloves and face paint just yet. Find someone to be your voice and use your gift to draw people to Jesus.

The purpose of this book is to encourage followers of Jesus Christ to open their mouths and personally proclaim the good news of salvation. From the outset, let me state that witnessing does not come naturally or easily to me. I fight against it and must really work at it. Like many of you, I would rather remain silent. Silence, however, is not an option. Not only is our silence a sinful rebellion against God's expressed will, it threatens to condemn countless millions of souls to a Christless hell.

When Ben-Hadad, King of Aram, was besieging Samaria (see 2 Kings 7), the resulting famine was horribly severe; subsequently, the people were at the point of starvation. Outside the city walls sat four leprous men—outcasts caught between the enemy and their disease. They were not allowed inside the walls to get what little food remained, and the enemy was closing in on them. These four desperate individuals decided to surrender to the army of Aram, hoping at least for a last meal before their execution as prisoners. When they approached the enemy camp, however, they discovered it deserted. The vast army's entire store of provisions was theirs for the taking. They filled their stomachs first, then carried away silver and gold and clothing items. These they hid before returning to repeat the process. It was on their second foray into the camp that their consciences arrested their attention. They looked at each other, weighed down under the burden of plundered goods, and said, "We are not doing right. This day is a day of good news, but we are keeping silent. . . . Now therefore come, let us go and tell the king's household" (2 Kings 7:9).

All the provisions of God's abundant grace are at our fingertips. Nothing has been withheld from us, yet we have grown spiritually fat and sassy, hoarding the goodness of God for ourselves as if it were a divine right that only we should enjoy. What we are doing is not right. We cannot keep it to ourselves any longer. We must open our hearts to those who are suffering under the siege of sin. We must open our mouths and report what we have found in Jesus Christ. The goal of our witness is communicating the good news to those who are lost in sin. As Alvin Reid writes, "Evangelism is the communication of the gospel by saved people to lost people."[4] A dying world is waiting to hear, but how will it hear when the majority of Christians are silent? Many have never attempted to give a verbal witness to a lost person.

The goal of our witness is not only that people hear but also that they understand what we say.

There are some strange approaches to evangelism being employed today that may, in the end, detract from the gospel rather than promote it. The giving of gospel tracts is a positive way to communicate the truths of God's Word, but we must be careful how we do this. If you place a tract on the table of a restaurant after eating, make sure you leave a good tip. A lousy tip will probably cause the server to discard the tract without even a glance. Another poor use of a tract is when the tract looks like money. Found money is a cause for rejoicing; finding it to be a fake in order to get you to read a tract borders on manipulation. By all means use tracts, but by all means take care as you do. When I give a tract, I try to do so with some word of encouragement accompanied by a smile and eye contact. The personal touch will increase the probability that the person will read the tract.

The giving of tracts does not relieve us of our calling to present a clear verbal witness. I once encountered a group that tried to spread the gospel in a way that required no speaking. A certain mission organization sent a representative to the 1992 Winter Olympics in France. They were a small outfit with an even smaller budget. They had purchased round-trip airfare for their "missionary" and tickets into some of the major Olympic events for this young man. They had no money for hotel accommodations and very little for food. I was in Albertville, together with several missionary colleagues, to lead a student witnessing team. One evening we received a frantic phone call from the secretary of this mission group in the United States. She cried and begged us to give their young minister a place to stay. The young man had come to France armed with one tool—a brightly colored sign on which was printed a Bible verse reference (not the verse itself, just its reference). I first noticed this type of ministry while watching athletic events, particularly golf, back in the United States. I had thought the man, sporting a multicolored, Afro-style wig, holding up a placard imprinted with a Bible reference, was just some fringe believer who wanted his fifteen minutes of fame. As it turned out, he was intentionally placed in a conspicuous location in order that the sign could be seen during the broadcast of the golf tournament.

Often in missions and evangelism, we talk about "target audience." This refers to the people we are trying to reach. We send missionaries to Europe, for example, not only to minister to the French or the Portuguese but also to different people groups living within the borders of France and Portugal. Or, here in the United States we support volunteers who go to the big cities to reach the street people, a segment of the yet unreached population of those cities. It appears that the target audience of this sign-holding mission group would be, of necessity, English reading sports enthusiasts. The Bible reference on their sign was printed in English and would be incomprehensible to anyone who did not know the English language. To Japanese or Indian or Arab viewers, that Bible reference would be nothing more than gibberish, the message imperceptible. Most would not even know it was a reference to the Bible. So, in reality, this sincere, humble young man who traveled thousands of miles to witness at the Olympics (he spoke no French by the way, and had no intention of doing anything other than holding up his sign), had a target audience that mainly resided back home in the United States. In fact, his tickets were for events and matches in which Americans were participating, televised by an American network. I truly do not intend to scorn an organization that clearly identifies itself with the cause of Christ. Some people have perhaps been reached in just this way. I do question the strategy though. Why spend thousands of dollars and place a young minister in jeopardy from a lack of funds, traveling to a foreign mission field for the purpose of witnessing back in America? There are more effective ways to proclaim the gospel.

We tend to forget the most obvious and best way to do missions and evangelism. We are called simply to speak Jesus into the world. Recently, while reading through the Gospel of Matthew, I was struck by how many times I found the words, "and Jesus said," or in the first person, "I say to you." Jesus spent His earthly ministry telling His disciples what they needed to know. Yes, He showed them as well, but He spent most of His time telling them. We are to emulate this pattern. We must speak if we want people to hear and understand. There is no shortage of gospel presentations or evangelism strategies. I learned on the mission field that in order to reach people I needed to try any and all approaches, but we will not reach our world for Christ by merely multiplying our programmed and impersonal presentations. Our world will not move toward faith in Jesus until every believer finds his or her voice and uses it to point others to the Savior.

The Shadow of Babel

We need to reconsider how we go about the task of winning the lost world to Christ. Whatever our mission field, we need to do a much better job of communicating Jesus Christ. Let me invite you to rethink your involvement in and commitment to spreading the gospel of Jesus Christ. May we learn again, or for the first time, to use our voices for the Lord Jesus. What a tremendous joy it is to speak the gospel and to lead someone to faith in Jesus.

Let me encourage you to take a moment or two at the end of each chapter to focus your attention on the "Increase Your Word Power" section. The suggestions there will help you learn Bible verses and key concepts that can be used in explaining the gospel to a lost person. Would you pray with me that God would raise up a mighty army of witnesses who will find their voices and boldly speak Jesus into their world?

CHAPTER ON E

THE WORDS OF GOD

When we speak in normal, everyday language, we seldom stop to think about the words we use. We are familiar with the rhythms and speech patterns of our quotidian communication. We are often oblivious to the regional grammatical errors that invade our speech. In special situations when we need to say something as precisely as possible, we do, in fact, pause and sometimes struggle to find the right word or phrase. But, generally speaking, we communicate without much conscious attention to words—they just flow.

Learning another language, however, is impossible without meticulous scrutiny being given to each and every word. Oh, the embarrassment I felt when, attempting to communicate one thought, I chose the wrong word and said something completely different. Once, with my wife sitting by my side in language class, I asked my female teacher to disrobe. When she laughed and pointed out the error of my word choice, I must have turned fifty shades of red.

A few years ago, my son and his future wife came home from college for a visit. Jaime had recently returned from a mission trip to London, England. She learned the hard way about the importance of saying the right words. Not realizing there was a dress code at one of the schools where her mission team ministered, she had dressed in a pair of dirty jeans (it was toward the end of their three-week trip and she had already worn all she had brought with her). When she got up to address the students, she felt bad for not meeting the dress code and apologized for her pants being dirty. She was greeted with roaring laughter. In England, "pants" refer to underwear. "Trousers" was the word she needed. I can certainly sympathize with her embarrassment.

Language learners often make two common mistakes. The first is poor word choice and the other is mispronunciation. We often fall prey to these mistakes in witnessing. By our choice of words, it is possible to make the good news sound like bad news. We can actually turn people away from Jesus by what we say and how we say it. Memorized gospel presentations are useful at this point because they help us pay attention to the words we employ. The danger of this approach is that we may say the words without emotion or conviction. To use such a witnessing tool effectively, we must make it our own so that it flows from our hearts and not just our minds (see Appendix: Personalize Your Gospel Presentation).

It is also possible to mispronounce the gospel. If we allow doctrinal errors or spiritual doubts into our communication of Christ, we can give a distorted view of God. Indeed, some of the most prolific door-to-door evangelists are those who are adherents of "a different gospel" (Galatians 1:6-7). Jehovah's Witnesses and Mormon missionaries come knocking at our doors under the pretense of enlightened truth, yet they mispronounce the gospel in blasphemous ways. We must be careful that we do not compromise the gospel as we use words to draw people to Jesus.

As we undertake our study of communicating Jesus Christ to the world, may we begin with God. We speak, because He has spoken. And He has never misspoken a single word.

The Bible details for us the story of God communicating himself to man. We call this revelation. God has revealed himself by telling us who He is and by reminding us what He has done. The Bible begins with these words: "In the beginning God created the heavens and the earth. . . . And God said . . ." (Genesis 1:1, 3 NIV). No less than eleven times in the first chapter of Genesis do we find the words, "And God said." We also find other words of speaking, such as "God called" and "God blessed." God's creative word initiated a world based upon fellowship and communication. Adam and Eve enjoyed an unhindered relationship with God, hearing "the sound of the LORD God as he was walking in the garden in the cool of the day" (Genesis 3:8 NIV).

Yet it was another sound, the hissing temptations of the evil one, which sent humanity spiraling downward into sin and self-destruction. At the impulse of that serpent, speech was used for the first time to convey half-truths and deception. Then, in fear of God's disapproval, the man and his wife crafted words to cast blame on each other and even upon God ("The woman *you* put here with me," Genesis 3:12 NIV, emphasis added). It was with stern words that God cursed His beautiful creation and sent the man and woman away from His presence.

Lest we think that words themselves are also under the curse along with the rest of creation, may we be reminded that God's redemptive call to Adam came via words: "Adam, where are you?" God has been calling out to mankind ever since. And with what urgent, spectacular words He calls us! "'Come now, and let us reason together,' says the LORD. 'Though your sins are as scarlet, they will be as white as snow; though they are red like crimson, they will be like wool'" (Isaiah 1:18). The Bible concludes with wonderful words of invitation: "The Spirit and the bride say, 'Come!' And let him who hears say, 'Come!' Whoever is thirsty, let him come; and whoever wishes, let him take the free gift of the water of life" (Revelation 22:17 NIV). God calls us back to himself with words and He desires to receive our spoken response. Hosea proclaimed, "Take words with you and return to the LORD. Say to him: 'Forgive all our sins and receive us graciously, that we may offer the fruit of our lips'" (Hosea 14:2 NIV). Indeed, redeemed humanity offers up to God words that have themselves been redeemed and renewed. The voice, once used for sinful purposes, can now be offered in praise to God. "Through Jesus, therefore, let us continually offer to God a sacrifice of praise—the fruit of lips that confess his name" (Hebrews 13:15 NIV).

God's voice, of course, is not limited to creation. Eighteenth century deists, elevating reason above revelation, believed that the world was like a clock and God the clockmaker. Creation complete, He wound up the clock and let it run without interference. If that were true, we would not have heard God's voice since His creative work was done. In other words, according to the deists, God spoke the world into being and then stopped speaking. We know this is not the case, however. He spoke to Noah, to Abraham, to Jacob, and to Moses, just to name a few. With Moses came a major shift in God's communication. Previously, God spoke to one man at a time, but now He desired to let everyone hear His voice. He had Moses gather all Israel at the base of Mt. Sinai, "And God spoke all these words . . ." (Exodus 20:1 NIV). What followed was the giving, in audible voice, of the Ten Commandments (see Deuteronomy 4:12; 5:4, 22). God was saying, "This is important. I want you all to hear." But the people could not bear to hear the voice of God. They begged Moses to be their mediator: "Speak to us yourself and we will listen. But do not have God speak to us or we will die" (Exodus 20:19 NIV).

So awesome was the voice of God that man could hardly endure it. Throughout the rest of the Old Testament, God chose to speak primarily through specially placed individuals like priests, prophets, and kings. Even though He restricted His audible voice—how it must have grieved Him not to vocalize His love for His people—He made His words known. Sadly, His words were often words of judgment to a rebellious people. The prophets spoke in authoritative tones: "Thus saith the LORD!" The voice was the prophet's; the words were the LORD's.

Perhaps because man paid so little attention to God's prophetic voice, God silenced His own. Malachi spoke for God and then . . . silence. For over four hundred years, God choked back any word of any kind. The silence spoke louder than the words and caused Israel to sit up and take notice. God's unspoken language of expectation prompted the people to long for Him again. Hearts were attentive and ears were tuned to what God might say. When the time was right, God broke His silence, dispatching angels with messages of hope: first to Zechariah, then to Mary and Joseph, and again to lowly shepherds. The air was filled with the words of God! Luke, in his Gospel, tells it this way: "The word of God came to John son of Zechariah in the desert. He went into all the country around the Jordan, preaching a baptism of repentance for the forgiveness of sins" (Luke 3:2-3 NIV). John was the "voice of one calling in the desert, 'Prepare the way for the Lord'" (Luke 3:4 NIV).

All of God's Old Testament words, the messages given by angels, and John's words were in preparation for the arrival of *The Word*, Jesus Christ. When God broke His silence, He really spoke. His voice was heard by any who would listen. Harkening back to God's creative words, the apostle John wrote, "In the beginning was the Word, and the Word was with God, and the Word was God. . . . And the Word became flesh, and dwelt among us" (John 1:1, 14). Now God's voice could not be mistaken. Jesus embodied the very words of God and spoke these words with truthful authority and loving wisdom.

On several occasions God's spoken words broke forth from heaven and showered down around the living Word, Jesus. At the waters of His baptism and again upon the Mount of Transfiguration, the voice boomed its thunderous message: "This is my Son!" God's audible voice speaking from heaven commanded that Jesus, the Word of God, be listened to intently.

Most of the world did not listen to Jesus, however, and the

voice of the mob prevailed. Once again, angry voices speaking half-truths and deception brought God's perfection to death. Thinking they were silencing God for good, ungodly men nailed the Word of God to a cross. But the voice was heard even from the cross. As a harbinger of worldwide evangelism, above the cross of Jesus the soldiers nailed a sign written in three languages, proclaiming Jesus as king. Jesus' cry, "It is finished!" shouted defeat to the enemies of God who could never again silence His voice.

With Jesus' ascension, that voice was withdrawn only to be replaced with another, internal voice that is heard not with ears but with hearts. That inner voice led Jesus' followers to open their mouths with joyous proclamations. Before His ascension, Jesus had commanded His disciples to use their voices to declare the gospel to the entire world. His resurrection gave power to their words. "We are witnesses" became their motto. Again, however, men who preferred silence and darkness tried to stop the message from spreading. Hateful words resounded to accuse and slander. God's messengers were shouted down, but when one voice fell silent, a choir of others sang out.

But even with the coming of the Holy Spirit at Pentecost, God had not finished speaking. That same Spirit inspired men to write down accounts of Jesus' life, death, and resurrection. They recorded the history of the beginning and growth of the church. Paul and other apostles wrote letters on how to live for Jesus. John received prophetic visions of God's final word on His creation. The apostle Peter described how this happened in 2 Peter 1:21: "Men spoke from God as they were carried along by the

Holy Spirit" (NIV). The result of these writings was a complete and full revealing of all that God wanted to say to man. Paul affirmed that "all Scripture is God-breathed" (2 Timothy 3:16 NIV). The author of Hebrews declared, "The Word of God is living and active" (4:12 NIV). The biblical invitation is to hear God's words and believe: "So faith comes from hearing, and hearing by the word of Christ" (Romans 10:17). John added that "these are written that you may believe that Jesus is the Christ, the Son of God, and that by believing you may have life in his name" (John 20:31 NIV).

Indeed, God has spoken! Because He has spoken, we too must speak. Jesus has promised help for our weak voices. He knows how tempted we are to silence ourselves, so He encourages us to witness with these words: "Do not worry about what to say or how to say it. At that time you will be given what to say, for it will not be you speaking, but the Spirit of your Father speaking through you" (Matthew 10:19-20 NIV). Jesus spoke this promise in the context of His followers being dragged before religious councils or civil courts to explain their actions and beliefs, but the promise is valid for all who would be bold enough to speak a word of witness in any situation. He has simply promised to strengthen our voice and enable our words so that we might proclaim the good news of Jesus Christ.

With this promise of powerful, overcoming words, Jesus commands us to speak. "What I tell you in the dark, speak in the daylight; what is whispered in your ear, proclaim from the roofs" (Matthew 10:27 NIV). When we speak the gospel empowered by the Holy Spirit, we are speaking the very words of God to a lost world. We become God's voice to those He is seeking.

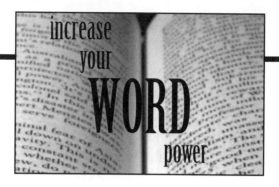

increase your **WORD** power

1   Read and memorize Romans 10:17: "So faith comes from hearing, and hearing by the word of Christ." What role did the Bible have in your own conversion experience? Who was instrumental in leading you to faith in Jesus Christ?

2   The Bible claims to be the authoritative Word of God. Do you live as if the Bible is authoritative over every aspect of your life? Do you read the Bible every day? Are you obeying it? In prayer, commit yourself to be a student of the Bible. Ask God to make it powerful in your life and through your life as you share it with others. Is there someone you can encourage to read the Bible? Is there someone with whom you can read the Bible on a regular basis?

3   If someone to whom you were witnessing was having a difficult time connecting the Bible's message to his or her life, you might share John 20:31. Read this verse and think about how you might use it to help such a person.

CHAPTER TWO

THE PROPHET'S CALL

People who know me today have a difficult time believing that I was a very shy child and teenager. Once, when I was about seven years old, a missionary came to the church my dad was pastoring. I was very impressed by the native costume he wore but also by his stature. At dinner after church, I wanted to know how tall he was, but I was much too afraid to ask that simple question. I begged my mom to ask him for me. She gently refused but said she would help. So we alternated words in what must have seemed a very strange interview: "How *tall* are *you?*" Two words were a mountain to me at that age.

When guests came to our house or I heard a knock at the door, I would scurry off to my room and hide under my bed. (It is amazing that I would crawl under that bed at all, since I was convinced something evil lived under there at night.) I just did not enjoy meeting new people or talking to those who I did not know.

I was still awkwardly shy when I went off to college. The Lord had just called me to preach (I will say more about that in a later chapter), but I was keeping it pretty much to myself. It took more than half of a seven-hour car ride to find the courage to tell my dad about my calling. We were on my way to register for classes at Southwest Baptist University in Bolivar, Missouri. There, I began my education as a math major—numbers were nonthreatening; people made me nervous. At the start of my second semester, I decided it was time to begin preparing for the ministry, so I changed my major to Religious Studies. At about the same time, I met and fell instantly in love with my future wife, Judy. My shyness was a huge obstacle to overcome in our relationship. If I could not ask a missionary how tall he was, how in the world could I ask a beautiful young woman to marry me?

When, after two or three weeks of dating, Judy asked her roommates what they thought of me, they shrugged their shoulders and replied, "We don't know. He never says anything!" Thinking that I was a rather arrogant snob who did not like them, they wrote me off. Little did they know the terror that overwhelmed me when confronted with new acquaintances and initial conversations. Judy assured them that I was not what they thought me to be. She became concerned, however, with my extreme shyness and asked me a very pointed question: "How can you be a preacher if you are afraid to talk?"

That question haunted me. I knew that God had called me to the ministry. What I had to come to terms with was that a call from God was a call to speak. This fact is true not only for those in professional ministry but also for all who profess faith in Jesus Christ. We have a calling from God to speak. As I read and studied, I realized that I had something in common with some of the reluctant prophets that I encountered in the Bible.

The call to prophetic service was, of necessity, a call to speak. When God met with Moses at the burning bush, He informed him that He was sending him back to Egypt to confront Pharaoh and to lead Israel to the Promised Land. Moses understood that this would require him to use his voice. Immediately, Moses complained to the Lord: "O LORD, I have never been eloquent, neither in the past nor since you have spoken to your servant. I am slow of speech and tongue" (Exodus 4:10 NIV). Funny, but it seems that Moses had little trouble finding the words to say as he tried to rationalize his way out of God's call. His final excuse was met by an awesome promise and a bold challenge: "Who gave man his mouth? Who makes him deaf or mute? Who gives him sight or makes him blind? Is it not I, the LORD? Now go; I will help you speak and will teach you what to say" (Exodus 4:11-12 NIV).

When I first read these verses as a young ministry student, I became hopeful that God would give me the ability to speak and the words to say. My faith grew and I gained confidence that I might indeed come out of my debilitating shyness. Moses was less convinced. His response to God's promise was, "O LORD, please send someone else to do it" (Exodus 4:13 NIV). The Lord became angry with him because of his refusal to be His mouthpiece. Rather than cast Moses aside, however, He sent Aaron, Moses' brother, to be his helper and spokesman.

God takes seriously our call to speak. How God's anger must burn against a generation of silent Christians! You cannot use the excuse that God has not placed a special call on your life. The New Testament clearly says God expects every believer to use his or her voice in witnessing to the lost. The call to follow Jesus is a call to speak. He will not send someone else in your place.

Moses was not the only reluctant prophet. God called Jeremiah at a considerably younger age than He did Moses. I can identify more with Jeremiah. Moses did not want to speak; Jeremiah did not know how: "Ah, Sovereign LORD, . . . I do not know how to speak; I am only a child" (Jeremiah 1:6 NIV). This was Jeremiah's surrendered response to the Lord's appointment to prophetic ministry. What a daunting call for a young man: "I have appointed you as a prophet to the nations" (1:5 NIV). Again, the command was to speak: "You must go to everyone I send you and say whatever I command you" (see Jeremiah 1:5-10 NIV).

When the Lord calls and commands, He gives us the ability to obey—even to speak. Jeremiah testifies to God's help, "Then the LORD reached out his hand and touched my mouth and said to me, 'Now, I have put my words in your mouth'" (Jeremiah 1:9 NIV). God gave Jeremiah a hard task—speaking to people who did not want to listen and who fought against both the Lord's words and Jeremiah's prophetic ministry. Jeremiah languished under his call, tried to suppress his voice, but found that he could not help but speak. At one point Jeremiah cried out, "Oh, my anguish, my anguish! I writhe in pain. Oh, the agony of my heart! My heart pounds within me, *I cannot keep silent*" (Jeremiah 4:19 NIV, emphasis added). His initial language is descriptive of the feeling many Christians have when they go out on church visitation and approach the front door of a prospect— "Oh the agony . . . my heart pounds within me." We hope and pray no one opens the door.

Try as we might, though, we cannot remain silent. There is

something, someone compelling us to speak. To keep silent is to resist the Holy Spirit's urgent prompting. The apostle Paul knew the inward swelling up of a message that must be conveyed. He wrote in 1 Corinthians 9:16, "For I am under compulsion; for woe is me if I do not preach the gospel." The word Paul used is not the word we usually associate with formal preaching as in a prepared sermon, but a word that is best translated as *evangelize*. Paul said that he was compelled to bear witness for Jesus. Like Jeremiah, he could not keep quiet. Believers today, however, have become experts at remaining silent. We have found better excuses than even Moses used. We have rationalized our silence and justified our disobedience. The greatest excuse of all is the one that brings solace to the reluctant witness. It goes something like this: "Why should I have to witness, that is what we pay the preacher for." We like Bible translations that have Paul say, "Woe is me if I do not preach," for most Christians are not called to preach in that sense of the word. To understand that Paul was not speaking about preaching from a pulpit on Sunday mornings, but about his day-to-day witness as a follower of Jesus, confronts our silence for what it is—sin!

The task of witnessing cannot be easily dismissed. Yes, God has called the professionals—pastors and ministers, evangelists and missionaries—to bear witness, but that in no way releases the average believer from the responsibility of speaking to others on Christ's behalf. It is true that the prophets were professionals—they were called to an office and a function. They were "preachers who communicated God's words in order to transform their audience's thinking and social behavior."[5] But they were also "real people attempting to communicate urgent messages to friends,"[6] family, fellow countrymen, and even to their enemies. I cringe in disappointment every time a church member calls me or gets me aside at church and says that they are concerned about a friend's lost condition and asks me to go see the person. The tragedy is that they believe they have done their duty by informing the minister. They have washed their hands of the burden. Now, if that person remains in a lost condition, it is the preacher's fault and not theirs. I can sense the Lord's anger burning as it did against Moses. If you have a burden for a lost friend or family member, do not lay it aside by putting it off onto someone else. If you have the burden, it is because God has given *you* the burden and the responsibility to act upon it. Find your voice and go witness to the one for whom you are burdened. You will most likely do a better job than the professionals because your words will be spoken from a burdened heart.

Most Christians sidestep this issue, however. God's people just are not concerned for the lost anymore. They seal off their hearts from lost friends, refusing even to think about the eternal consequences of being separated from God. Many Christians will not let their hearts be burdened. We need to recapture the passion of Jeremiah and of Paul. When our heavy hearts begin to writhe in anguished pain over the desperate condition of the lost, we will find our voice, but not until then. So with this in mind, let us review what Jesus said about the lost condition.

It is no surprise that Jesus had more to say about hell than He did heaven. He came to save people from an eternity in hell. In Mark 10:45, Jesus says that He came "to give his life a ransom for many." His was a rescue mission, saving people from the horrors of hell. When speaking to Zaccheus in Luke 19:10, He said, "For the Son of Man has come to seek and to save that which was lost." He used a word that He also used when speaking to Nicodemus. These two men were on the far extremes of life in first century Israel. Nicodemus was a Pharisee, a spiritual leader of the nation; Zaccheus sold out to Rome and collected taxes for the enemy of the Israelites. Both men suffered under the same condition. They were lost and in danger of perishing. In John 3:16, Jesus said, "Whoever believes in him shall not perish, but have eternal life." The term *perish* here and the term *lost* in Luke 19 are from the same Greek word stem and reference the same terrifying condition. *Lost* is a composite of a prefix that means "away from" and the verb form "to destroy." Together they mean "to perish." To be without Jesus Christ is to be lost and perishing. To be lost is to face the present with what Roy Fish calls a *moral insanity*:

> Many of those who are lost, do they not act as if they are frightened at the very prospect of being saved? They will do everything possible to keep from being saved. They regard damnation as if it were salvation. And they live as if salvation were damnation. They rush to damnation as if it were heaven. They run from salvation as if it were hell. That is moral madness, moral insanity. A lost person will reject Jesus and press with fury down the way to hell as if it were the chief good of his existence. All the while they evade the way to heaven as if it were the worst possible thing that could happen.[7]

Not only is there this terrible present condition, but the word also speaks to a horrific eternal destiny. It means to be ever dying but never reaching the release of death. The lost person's final condition is to experience the horrors of dying without any hope of it ending. This is why Jesus often used words like "weeping and gnashing of teeth" to describe this condition. He said hell was a place of eternal punishment and called it "outer darkness" (Matthew 25:30).

Jesus' most telling words about humankind's lost condition are found in Luke 16:19-31. There, He spoke of the plight of the rich man who lived without fear of God in this life only to be confronted with the horrors of an eternity without hope in the next. Jesus said this man was in torment and agony. Jesus left no question as to the duration of this agony: "And besides all this, between us and you a great chasm has been fixed, so that those who want to go from here to you cannot, nor can anyone cross over from there to us" (Luke 16:26 NIV). I am guessing that one day many Christians will wish to go from here (heaven in Jesus' story in Luke 16) to loved ones and friends who are in agony in hell, but they will not be able to—God's judgment has fixed a great, impassable chasm. The time to be concerned about the lost is while they are still living, while there is still opportunity to speak the good news to them.

We must embrace this call to speak. No excuse may be proffered that will discharge us from this responsibility before God. Even my problem of shyness was not a valid reason to refuse to speak. Paul urged his young protégé, Timothy, to be bold, exhorting him to move beyond his diffidence: "For God did not give us a spirit of timidity, but a spirit of power, of love and of self-discipline" (2 Timothy 1:7 NIV).

Paul taught Timothy what he already knew from his own experience—to shrink back from the gospel's urgent message is to deny the Lord Jesus himself. Our silence betrays our claim to faith. It betrays Jesus Christ. Judas betrayed Jesus with a kiss; we betray Him with our silence. In the book of Romans (see 1:16 and 10:14), Paul says, "I am not ashamed of the gospel, because it is the power of God for the salvation of everyone who believes. . . And how can they believe in the one of whom they have not heard? And how can they hear without someone preaching to them" (NIV).

Can we, like Paul, claim to be unashamed? Hardly! If we are to become the bold witnesses that we are called to be, we must deal with the issue of shame. Many believers remain silent because at the heart of the matter they are ashamed of Jesus Christ. It is not popular today to be a follower of Jesus Christ. After the events of September 11, 2001, it became popular to speak about faith in God. It did not take long for true believers to realize that to speak of God in generic terms was fine, but to speak of Jesus was too much. American society simply does not want us to speak about Jesus. We did not need anything else to discourage us, but now it is easier not to identify with Jesus by our words. Not wanting to look the fool, we remain silent. Does Jesus not mean enough to us that we would be willing to claim allegiance to Him verbally? Are we reluctant to use our voice for Jesus because we are afraid of what people might think or say? Would we rather stay in the good graces of our neighbors and friends than to speak up for the Lord Jesus Christ? These are tough questions, but our silence carries with it dire consequences. Jesus could not conceive of the possibility of a silent Christian. He said, "Whoever acknowledges me before men, I will also acknowledge him before my Father in heaven. But whoever disowns me before men, I will disown him before my Father in heaven" (Matthew 10:32-33 NIV). Our silence ought to cause us to call into question whether we have truly given our hearts to Jesus. Now, Jesus is not saying, and I am not implying, that a failure to witness will cause a person to lose his or her salvation, but He is saying that a true believer *will* witness. The mark of a follower of Jesus Christ is the use of the voice to witness to the lost. The call to follow Jesus is a call to speak.

Christian, have you grown comfortable in your silence? Witnessing *is* your responsibility. It *is* your calling. May we repent of our silence and begin to speak for Jesus. Let me suggest a prayer of repentance:

> *Lord Jesus, I am not ashamed of you or the gospel even though I have been acting like it. Forgive me for remaining silent. Give me a renewed burden for those who are lost without you. Grant me the courage and boldness to use my voice for you. May your Holy Spirit provide opportunities to witness and give me the words to say. I will be your witness. In your name, I pray. Amen.*

Then to ask God to rekindle an evangelistic flame in your heart, you might want to use this poetic prayer penned by Roland Q. Leavell:

Oh, for a passionate passion for souls!
Oh, for a pity that yearns!
Oh, for a love that loves unto death!
Oh, for a fire that burns!

Oh, for prevailing power in prayer
That pours itself out for the lost;
Victorious prayer in the Saviour's name!
Oh, for a Pentecost![8]

Now that we have brought our sinful silence to the Lord in prayer and abandoned it there with Him, let me say a word or two about the relationship between the Holy Spirit and our voices (see also chapter 10). The Holy Spirit's presence in our lives urges us to speak. He inhabits every true believer and presses every true believer to the duty of using his or her voice in witness. This is his role. Jesus said, "You will receive power when the Holy Spirit comes on you; and you will be my witnesses" (Acts 1:8 NIV). The apostle Paul declares that the result of the filling of the Holy Spirit is speech. "Be filled with the Holy Spirit. Speak . . ." (Ephesians 5:18-19 NIV).

When God calls us to do something, He always gives us the resources and the ability to carry it out. Our call to follow Jesus is, indeed, a call to speak. He is faithful; He has given us His Holy Spirit who inspires our voices and guides our speech. When Elijah was transported by chariot into God's presence, Elisha, taking up his mantle, continued and enlarged upon his prophetic ministry. Who in our generation will take up the mantle of witness and go forth in strong and undeterred voice to proclaim Jesus Christ?

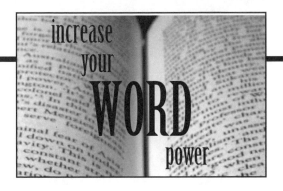

increase your WORD power

1   First Peter 3:15 says, "But in your hearts set apart Christ as Lord. Always be prepared to give an answer to everyone who asks you to give the reason for the hope that you have" (NIV). A paraphrase of this verse might go like this: "Since Jesus is Lord of your life, always be ready to speak for him." Is Jesus on the throne of your life? Are you speaking for Him? Meditate upon the words "always" and "everyone." Do you have an *always* and *everyone* mentality when it comes to being a witness?

2   Paul told Timothy to "be prepared in season and out of season" (2 Timothy 4:2). Are you always ready to speak for Jesus, even when it may not be particularly convenient for you?

3   Pray that God would give you a deep burden for those who are lost. Begin praying every day for at least one lost person you know. Write down the name of at least one lost person that you know:

_____.

Pray that the Holy Spirit would give you an opportunity to share your faith today.

CHAPTER THREE

THE GIFT OF LANGUAGE

I found myself at the bottom of a long staircase that descended into an inner courtyard of the *Chateau de Versailles.* Versailles is the ornate castle of the kings Louis of France. King Louis XIV built it and King Louis XVI lost his head over it. It is immense. Its rooms are impeccably decorated with the richest and finest of materials. Secret passageways are hidden behind its tapestries and plastered walls. Inside its mirrored hallways and chandeliered sitting rooms, objects of great value and national heritage are on display for the world to see. A chapel and private opera house were provided for kings and queens and their guests. Today, daily tours lead wide-eyed foreigners through its complicated labyrinth of chambers. Tourists can pay for a guided history lesson in several languages. French, English, and German guides open the world of eighteenth-century France to all who will listen. I have never seen the whole thing.

I was escorted out halfway through the tour. One of those tour guides took me by the arm, opened one of those secret passageways, led me to the top of a staircase, and, pointing to the bottom, told me in stern but broken English to go wait there. So, with my infant son in my arms, I descended into the depths of embarrassment. It was all just a big misunderstanding. Besides, it is really my mother-in-law who should take the blame. My wife's parents had come for a visit and she wanted to see Versailles. So, we loaded up the kids and off we went.

It was a beautiful summer day. The gold-overlaid gate at the entrance of the property glistened in the brilliant sunlight, set against a backdrop of the clearest and bluest of skies imaginable. Every tourist in the country must have been there that day. The lines were agonizingly long, especially when you are trying to hold on to two rambunctious children and a toddler who had just discovered he could run. The line for the English tour was the longest. The estimated delay was nearly two hours. The German line was nearly as long, but so what? We did not speak German. Ah, but Judy and I did speak French! We had been given a special gift—the gift of language. The line for the French language tour was very short. We convinced our parents that we would translate the important information and that they could still enjoy the tour. We paid our fee and in we went. The sights were more than amazing. Gold-ornamented pieces of antiquity were all around us. Our guide was well-versed, but soon we realized he was much too well-versed. We concluded that he rather liked the sound of his own voice. He rambled on and on, giving every detail and every nuance of meaning possible. By the second stop of the tour, an upstairs bedroom, other groups began to pass us. They had broad smiles as they listened to short summaries and then moved on. We stood endlessly and labored under our guide's arrogant tones.

Like all the other groups, we had been given the rules before we started our tour. Rules number one, three, and five stated,

"No changing of groups!" Forty-five minutes into the tour, we had only advanced to the third room out of twenty or so. We saw a breach in the prison wall, however, and seized the opportunity to escape. A rather small English-speaking group came into the same room our group was occupying, and the two guides relayed their information simultaneously. As they spoke, I nudged my wife, and we devised a plan. Judy, her parents, Joshua and Nathan would slowly edge their way over to the English group. My in-laws were already leaning that way, since they understood what the guide was saying. When that group left, my family left with them as if they had always been part of that tour. As a cover, I stayed with the French-speaking group along with my toddling son, Matthieu.

The plan worked beautifully. Our guide was so enamored with his nation's history as told with his melodious voice that he never noticed that my family had broken free. Thirty minutes later, however, I had only moved ahead one room. My arms ached from holding my son. I grew weary and fatigued. My head began to spin and I unwisely decided to make a break of my own. I reasoned that my guide would think that my son had a dirty diaper or some other problem. In fact, I do not think he noticed my departure. I also figured that I could catch up to the rest of my family and enjoy the remainder of the tour. I was sorely mistaken. I had calculated that only one group had passed mine since my wife's escape. All I had to do was manage to pass that one group and I would be home free, reunited with my loved ones. To my surprise, though, after I had successfully navigated past that one group, I met another different group. I was confused.

Later, I concluded that my wife's adopted group was breezing past others as it had ours at first.

I pressed on past that group of German speakers and advanced through two more unoccupied rooms but still had not found my family. I was now more than just a little lost, thinking that somehow I had wandered off the route of the tour. I had no choice but to double back and try to attach myself discretely either to an English-speaking group or to my original French-speaking unit. It was on that return expedition that I got caught. The guide, a plumpish, stereotypical German woman, realized that I was lost and confused and clearly in violation of rules one, three, and five. She forcefully grabbed my arm and sent me scurrying off to Versailles' version of Siberia. She knew English well enough to humiliate me thoroughly as she told me where to go and how to get there. So, there I was at the bottom of a long staircase in an inner courtyard of the *Chateau de Versailles*. Tour over. No refund!

Confusion can prove embarrassing. Imagine the reaction of the laborers building that ancient architectural masterpiece, the tower of Babel, when they woke one morning to discover that they could no longer understand one another. So profound was the impact of this failure of communication that they ceased working. Those who were given similar languages gathered together and migrated to some place to call their own. Eventually those of different languages would become their enemies as they vied for political position in the world. One language plus one people equaled no need for God. To show His creation how much it needed Him, God confused the language of the whole world and scattered them like chaff thrown to the wind.

Some "enlightened" people today believe that the future of missions in this culturally diverse and multilinguistic world of ours is a return to Babel. "Everyone understands English now" is the oft-repeated mantra. Nobody who has traveled outside of the United States would believe it, though. You can find some places even within the borders of our land where one would wonder if English is understood.

If we are to win our world to Christ Jesus, we must do it through the medium of language. And if we are serious about unreached peoples, we must do it through languages that are rather difficult to learn. No universal language will make this arduous task any easier. Returning to Babel would not prove successful. Pentecost, not Babel, is the key. God is in the business of giving the gift of language.

The events of the day of Pentecost are recorded in the second chapter of Acts. That passage is reputed to be the impetus for what has become known as speaking in tongues or *glossolalia*. Whatever one may say about "tongues," that is definitely not the subject of Acts, chapter 2. The miracle of Pentecost was language, many languages, spoken and heard so that communication was unhindered in any way. God had given the gift of language.

There is a vitally important principle that is gleaned from the details of the day of Pentecost. This principle proceeds from the very heart of God and challenges every believer to be a language learner. Why would God use a special gift of speaking and/or hearing on that day? Why did He not just give the message in

Hebrew or Aramaic? Most of those gathered in the streets of Jerusalem were Jews of the Diaspora. Surely, they were familiar with the Hebrew language. Indeed, they probably were, but it is just as probable that Hebrew was not their heart language. Many of these dispersed Jewish families had lived outside of Israel for hundreds of years.

Heart language is the language of thoughts and emotions and intimate communication. The French language is considered by many to be the language of romance and love, but when I wanted to speak intimately with my wife while we were missionaries, I spoke English, our heart language. You see, every person has the God-given right to hear the good news of Jesus Christ in his or her native language. The gospel, to be properly understood, must be communicated in the heart language of the hearer. This is important for several reasons. What is at stake is the eternal destiny of individual souls. Should we expect someone to make such a weighty decision having heard the explanation of benefits and the dangers of refusal only in a secondary language? Every person has the right to hear these eternal truths in the language that they immediately and fully comprehend. Again, since such a call to repentance and faith involves not only a person's intellect but also his emotions and will, only the language of the heart will enable the person to understand thoroughly and surrender his entire being to the Lordship of Jesus.

God validated the worth of every person on that glorious day of Pentecost. He was, in effect, saying, "This is important. I want each of you to hear it, not through a muffled and garbled secondary language, but with your hearts and minds fully engaged."

What does this mean for those of us who aspire to be better witnesses? Accepting the principle that every person has the right to hear the gospel in the language of his or her heart, we, then, must learn to speak that language. If we are called to be international missionaries or to minister to ethnic groups in America, then we must dedicate ourselves to learning another language, the language of our target group, and learn it well enough so that we may communicate correctly the truths of Scripture.

Upon completion of language study, my wife and I were linked to an established church in France in an apprenticeship with a French-speaking pastor. The purpose of this was to give us time to mature in our language use and to understand more fully the work of French Baptists. The pastor I worked with was an Englishman, but his French was impeccable. We communicated in French at all times. One day, as we discussed the sermon I was working on, he stopped reading what I had written and said, "Are you sure you want to say it this way. This is heresy." Immediately, I called time out and asked if we could speak in English for a minute. In my native language, I was better able to explain what I meant and the crisis was over. The pastor helped me adjust what I was saying in French so that I expressed sound doctrine. Beyond the initial embarrassment of having my theology challenged, the real issue was communicating the gospel in another language in such a way that it spoke truth to those who would hear me. This was a valuable lesson in my language acquisition. Believe me, from that day forward I was very careful in what I said and how I said it.

Woody D. Wilson

This lesson is important even if we are called to speak primarily to those who are like us here at home. We still must be language students. We must take care in what we say and in how we speak, paying attention to the words we use in conversation with others. We must seek to connect through language with the heart, mind, and will of our hearers.

Let's face it, Christians and non-Christians speak different languages. As followers of Jesus, we have adopted a new vocabulary and learned specialized terms. The deeper we grow in our relationship with the Lord, the more unique that language becomes. On the other hand, unbelievers use words and phrases that we have probably discarded when we accepted Jesus as our Savior. Even beyond the words employed, a great difference exists in the content of conversations. The mood of those conversations is dissimilar as well. One can see this most clearly when discussions center upon problems or illnesses. For the Christian, hope, peace, and faith filter into our speech at times like these. A quiet trust in the midst of difficult circumstances seeks to find God's good out of the intolerable. For the nonbeliever, however, the same conversations will be permeated with anger, bitterness, confusion, doubts, and complaints about the inequity of such events. We really do not speak the same language. I am not saying that we must adopt their vocabulary or the content of their conversations, but we must speak in ways that they can understand. Our theological terms, churchy words and Christian clichés will not hit the mark. We must envelop our deep faith in Jesus in words and phrases that they can identify with and understand.

One way we can do this is by speaking to them where they hurt. When crisis or tragedy strikes a person's life, the mind and heart converge upon that point. Everything else revolves around that pressing need. People are most open to listen to biblical truth when their lives are screaming for help. During these times, we can speak the language of their heart, ministering to their needs. If we are not careful, though, we can turn people away from the Lord by our words.

Christian people say some ridiculous-sounding statements at the worst possible times. The same statement said only in the presence of believers would most likely draw a nod of the head or a softly spoken amen, but when launched upon an unbeliever it assaults the ears and deepens the hurt. Let me give an example. At the wake of a woman who leaves behind a nine-year-old son, a seven-year-old daughter, and a husband who has lost the love of his life, a well-meaning Christian woman, in an attempt to convey comfort, says to the grieving husband, an unchurched man, "You might not understand why this happened, but God had His reasons. Somehow, this is His perfect will for your family. You will understand it better by and by." Then, turning to the sobbing children, the devout believer adds, "God must have needed your mommy in heaven." What this believer was probably trying to convey is that God is certainly able to work good out of horrible circumstances in our lives. She ended up speaking words that only confuse and embitter. That man and his children, who never attend church, must reason, "If it is God's will for my wife to die and leave me alone and if He wants her in heaven more than we need her here with us, then God must be insensitive and uncaring." The Christian wanted to express hope in eternal life and trust in God's mysterious ways, but the heart-broken family members come away thinking they want nothing to do with God.

Here is a better response to the family's grief, one that speaks their language: "Your wife's death is tragic and I'm so sorry. I don't understand why this had to happen. I know you will miss her deeply. The Bible teaches that when we hurt, Jesus is able to empathize with our hurts. He loves you, and I will be praying for you. If there is anything we at the church can do for you, please let us know." This message helps the man and his children know that they are not alone and that there are people who care and want to help. These statements also open a door for future ministry and witness.

We must strive, at all times, to speak in ways that people can hear and understand. Our goal is to so present Jesus Christ that people wrap their hearts and minds around Him and surrender their will to His lordship. They can only do this when we have communicated Jesus in the language of their hearts. The ability to do this, whether in other dialects and languages or in our own, is God's gift of language. It is a gift He gives to others through us.

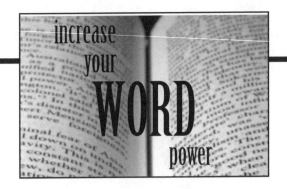

1 Read Acts 1:8 several times. What has God promised you in this verse? Will God ever leave you helpless or powerless when He asks you to witness to someone?

2 Once, a man asked Jesus, "Who is my neighbor?" The question centers upon the sphere of our responsibility. Ask yourself, "For whom am I responsible?" Think about your field of influence—your mission field. How far does it extend? Remember, there are lost persons that only you may be able to reach.

3 In prayer, ask God to place at least one lost person upon your mind and to help you connect with that person. Learn to speak his or her heart language. Speak Jesus to some need in his or her life.

CHAPTER FOUR

INTERPRETERS

The mission volunteer met the two young men at the front door of the church. She spoke in excited tones and was eager to share her news. She was part of a mission team from the United States, and the two young men had just arrived from England to help us in an intensive week of witnessing and revival meetings. Maybe she was just happy to find someone who understood English, but she could not remain silent. Before greetings were exchanged or introductions made, she rather joyously blurted out, "I've got a boil on my back. Would you like to see it?"

I am not sure if those young Brits ever recovered from that encounter. I can still see their bewildered expressions as they searched for the proper response to such an invitation. All week long, my wife and I listened as our guest instructed us on special diets and exotic purgings. I had the unenviable task of translating what she said to the French people with whom she came into contact. She is probably not aware that I purposefully did not give a word-for-word translation. I just could not bring myself to inform my dear French friends of all her medical ailments.

The greatest challenge, however, was yet to come. She decided that she wanted to share her testimony during the worship service on the last night of our weeklong series of evangelistic meetings. Without much forethought and with even less organizational ability, she launched into a rambling, nonchronological, dissertation-length exposé of her life. The centerpiece of her "testimony" was her struggle to cope with all her numerous misfortunes and, oh yes, the boil on her back was mentioned (but not fully translated).

The most difficult task we have as witnesses is to interpret properly Jesus, His life, and His teachings to a world that does not understand. Every unbelieving person has the need of someone to explain the truths of Scripture. Philip, one of the seven chosen to serve the needs of widows in Acts 6, better known as Philip, the evangelist, joined himself to a chariot carrying an Ethiopian eunuch. This man was an official of Queen Candace and had been to Jerusalem to worship. Somehow, he came away from the City of David with a copy of the scroll of the prophet Isaiah. When the Holy Spirit led Philip to approach his chariot, the eunuch was reading from this scroll of Scripture. Overhearing him as he read, Philip asked a piercing question: "Do you understand what you are reading?"

The eunuch's response in Acts 8:31 (NIV) has echoed through the ages: "How can I [understand] unless someone explains it to me?" Philip was right where God wanted him to be—in between a lost seeker and a saving God. It is evident that the Holy Spirit was already at work upon the eunuch's heart and mind. So, what was Philip's role? Interpretation—that is, "someone to explain." The word that Luke uses as he records this encounter is a term that means to guide or lead. An interpreter is one who guides another person to a greater comprehension of the subject being discussed. In the case of an evangelistic witness, we are interpreters or guides, helping another person find his or her way toward God's offer of salvation.

At this point in the story, Philip did an amazing thing. He "began with that very passage of Scripture and told him the good news about Jesus" (Acts 8:35 NIV). That passage from Isaiah 53 does not mention Jesus by name, yet to us who believe it is abundantly clear that He is indeed the fulfillment of all those prophetic statements. It is clear to us because of Philip, in part. He understood that Jesus' sacrificial, atoning death was the subject of Isaiah's prophecy and he interpreted the passage in light of Jesus' cross experience. Without an interpreter, the eunuch would not have understood what he was reading.

We assume too much when we talk to most nonbelievers. We assume that they have at least a rudimentary, Primary-Sunday-School-Class understanding of the gospel. We assume that they are familiar with the most often-told Bible stories. We assume that they believe in God and think the Bible is the inspired Word of God. We assume that they are interested in spiritual things. We assume too much. There was a day, not so long ago chronologically, but light years philosophically, when the average American was interested in and knew the stories of the Bible. There was a day when most people knew deep down within them that there was a spiritual void in their lives and that only a commitment to the Lord could fill it.

My father was born in 1929. He grew up in church. His father was what we call today a bivocational pastor. My grandfather worked for the Missouri Pacific Railroad throughout the week and pastored/preached on the weekends. I grew up hearing stories about wonderful revival meetings where the church house was full to overflowing. Most of the time the sin-hardened men would not come into the church building, but they would listen to the sermon through the open windows. My dad told of times when the Spirit would move during the altar call and some lost man under deep conviction of sin would leave his perch under the window, open the doors of the church, and come down the aisle to the altar, where he was gloriously saved.

Times have changed. Lost people do not sit under our church windows any more. They are resistant to the promptings of the Holy Spirit. They do not understand what the Bible is or what it means. We cannot assume that they believe the Bible reveals God's truth. We can assume, however, that God is still at work, drawing people to himself. God is in the business of meeting people where they are. This He did through Philip. Philip began where the eunuch was, seeking to understand a passage of Isaiah. That is the role of an interpreter. We are called to meet people where they are and help them understand their need and God's gift of salvation.

Even though the words are sometimes used interchangeably, *translation* and *interpretation* have different emphases. *Translate* means to give the sense or equivalent of a word or text in another language; to change into another language. *Interpret* carries the idea of giving the meaning of, to explain or make clear, to elucidate. In Webster's Dictionary, the second definition of *translate* is to interpret; likewise, the fourth definition of *interpret* is to translate. As witnesses, we are called upon to do both. Even if we never learn or converse in a foreign language, we must translate ideas and concepts. For example, an adult sometimes must give the sense of a complicated word, phrase, or sentence in terms that a child can understand, translating from adult language to the language of a child. When I counsel with children concerning salvation, I always use a different set of words than I do with adults (even though the meaning is the same). Therefore, as we translate ideas and thoughts, we are acting as interpreters for those to whom we speak. They will understand what is being conveyed through the agency of our words. When sharing ideas that are difficult to grasp, we do not just find a synonym for the problem word (translation); we explain the meaning of the word (interpretation).

When my wife and I were in language school, all our classes were conducted in the French language. By contrast, many high school language classes use the English language as the base for learning. Students learn vocabulary by way of translation (i.e., maison = house, etc.). In language school, we were completely submerged in the French language. Out textbooks were written in French, our teachers spoke only French, only French was permitted to be spoken by the students in class, and our homework was entirely in French. I can remember looking up a word in the French dictionary and, subsequently, finding it necessary to look up three or four words of the definition. This was a time-consuming process, but the practice built my vocabulary more quickly. In truth, I was both translating and interpreting. Together, these two enable a greater understanding of a subject.

The Shadow of Babel

Most evangelism courses spend some time dealing with theological terms. The New Testament is replete with such words as justification, sanctification, regeneration, etc. The average lost person has little or no concept of these terms. Even smaller words such as saved or lost might not be readily understood. Our task is to translate these terms into words that can be easily grasped, interpreting the theological concept behind the words.

There is a real danger that in our attempt to interpret, what we actually do is interpolate. *Interpolate* means to alter some idea by the insertion of new and unauthorized matter, to put something different or irrelevant into, to corrupt. We must take great care in our interpretation that we do not corrupt the original concept. Nevertheless, this has occurred countless times. In simple terms, interpolation of the gospel is "watering it down." We weaken the call to commitment as we make it more palatable. Are the words of Jesus too harsh? Interpolate and make them mean something that Jesus never intended. Interpolation is the breeding ground of heresy.

We, then, must be truthful translators and interpreters with integrity. This is a high and holy calling. To translate from one language into another requires insight into both languages. Likewise, to translate Jesus to an unbeliever we need insight into both the nature of Jesus and the nature of man apart from God. We simply will not find our voice of witness until we contemplate the uniqueness of Jesus in juxtaposition to the lostness of man. If we contemplate neither Christ nor the lostness of man, we lose sight of the greatness of a Savior who desires nothing less than the eternal salvation of the lost. We also lose sight of the horrible condition of a soul in danger of eternal separation from God. A good translator/interpreter of the gospel has a heart full of devotion toward Christ Jesus and a deep burden for those who are lost in sin. By the act of interpretation, we are bringing the life, ministry, and words of Jesus to bear upon a sin-ruined life. By the same act, we are also escorting that lost soul to the threshold of heaven. There, by way of our translation and interpretation, the sinner finds the Savior and understands God's offer of salvation and receives it with joy.

While on the mission field, I always found it easier to translate from English into French rather than vice versa. I could more readily take the English I knew so well and find the French equivalent. When called upon to translate from French into English, I would struggle to find the right English words to convey the French thought. I often found myself repeating the French words to English-speaking guests. This underlines the importance of direction in translation. As witnesses, we move in a man-ward direction—that is, from Jesus to the lost person. We are not called upon to interpret some friend to Jesus. He already knows the person fully. Our task is to use our voices to interpret Jesus to those who do not understand Him or know Him. Let us keep moving in the direction of the lost. The Savior compels us to go and explain the gospel.

I left my office just minutes after completing the preceding paragraph. I had an appointment to meet with a man who is struggling to hold his family and his life together. He has been to prison and is now on probation; his demons have a firm hold on him. He has attended church services with his family but only on a limited basis. He is not truly conversant with theological topics. On the way to meet with him, I was thinking about what I had written just minutes before. I am standing between a lost sinner and a saving God. My task is to interpret the gospel message to this man so that he might understand and accept God's free gift of forgiveness and eternal life. The man told me how he had started drinking when he was twelve years old and how he wished he could move away from the bad influences around him and start over again. I seized upon that expressed wish and talked with him about what it means to be "born again." To be honest, I hesitated to put it into those terms because the phrase "born again" has been overused and abused. After President Carter boldly used this phrase to explain his salvation experience, the media had a heyday with it. Later, the pornographer Larry Flynt claimed to have had a "born again" experience after he was shot, but he soon returned to his pornographic ways, helping to confuse the true meaning of the word.

Would the man sitting across from me comprehend this phrase if I used it in our conversation? I decided that he would only if I interpreted it to him. I explained how Jesus spoke of being born again when in conversation with Nicodemus, who was a spiritual leader of Israel. Nicodemus had great difficulty in understanding what Jesus meant, so Jesus explained it to him further (see John 3:1-21). The man with whom I was talking was no spiritual giant like Nicodemus, but his need was just as great. He needed to know that he could have a fresh start in life. His sins could be forgiven and he could be born again. I shared 2 Corinthians 5:17 which says "if anyone is in Christ, he is a new creation; the old has gone, the new has come!" (NIV). He appeared to be intently listening to what I was telling him. My words were offering him hope that his life could change for the better by the power of God at work in him.

I gave the man a gospel tract to reinforce what we had been talking about and encouraged him to read it before he went to bed for the night. I said a prayer for him and he ran off to catch the ride that was waiting for him. Was I a good interpreter today? Only time will tell. In fact, I do not believe that my interpreting task is over. I will need to follow up with this man and continue to explain to him the teachings of the Bible. My prayer is that the Holy Spirit will take the words I shared with him and press them upon his mind and heart. I pray that he will truly be born again.

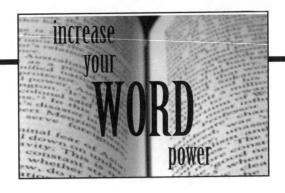

increase your **WORD** power

1   Jesus said to Nicodemus, "Truly, truly, I say to you, unless one is born again he cannot see the kingdom of God" (John 3:3). Nicodemus did not understand what Jesus meant. What would you say to someone who asked you to explain what "born again" means?

2   Think about how Jesus explained this concept to Nicodemus in John 3:5-8. Jesus emphasized a spiritual birth that leads to transformation. In your Bible, circle the word Spirit in these verses. Meditate upon the role of the Holy Spirit in the process of being born again.

3   Think about some occasions when people might talk about wanting a fresh start (i.e., New Year's resolution, divorce, graduation, work transfer, etc.). How could you turn these conversations to Jesus and the need to be born again?

CHAPTER FIVE

SO MANY VOICES

Do you remember the worst day of your life? That day is most likely etched into your memory in such a way that you can recall every detail as if it just happened. I have experienced several such days—like the day the doctor confirmed that our oldest son, then twelve years old, had diabetes. My heart broke into a thousand pieces that day. I argued with God, asking, "Why him? Why not me?"

The day I officially was no longer a missionary to France ranks up there among the worst. I felt like a failure. Even though I had struggled through many conflicting emotions, had prayed through to God's answer, and knew that our departure from missionary service was God's will for us, I still was overwhelmed by a sense of having failed my calling. Since that day, by many convincing proofs, God has affirmed our place in His service. I do not pretend that I understand it all and I admit there are times when I wish I was still on the mission field, but I believe that in this moment of time I am where God wants me to be.

Two experiences during our missionary orientation at the Missionary Learning Center in Rockwall, Virginia, would qualify as bad days. The leaders of our missionary training purposefully placed us as newly commissioned personnel into settings that challenged and instructed us. The first experience was a visit to a Jewish synagogue in Richmond. We attended one of their services to observe and learn. The rabbi planned a reception afterward, allowing us to mingle and converse with his people. That time of fellowship was pleasant and informative, but the worship service itself troubled me. The rabbi took the opportunity of our presence (we were a group of about fifty) to attack our faith and to ridicule Jesus. He told jokes as if he were a stand up comedian—jokes that mocked and scorned my Lord and Savior. His congregants would howl with laughter with each joke. I am certain that he wanted to destroy our faith and show it to be misdirected. I wept during that service as I thought about the scorn Jesus faced the day he was crucified. And yet today His own people continue to scoff and ridicule him. How true Scripture is when it says, "He was in the world, and though the world was made through him, the world did not recognize him. He came to that which was his own, but his own did not receive him" (John 1:10-11 NIV). I returned to the Missionary Learning Center with a heavy heart and a burdened soul.

I had hardly recovered from those shock waves of antagonism when we entered two charter buses early one morning and drove to the compound of a cultish group, existing under the name of the Lotus Community. We spent the day with the truth-starved followers of a bearded guru who claimed to be the answer to all the diverse religious teachings in the world. Supposedly, he had harmonized the major world religions into a cohesive and unified system of belief. While there, we ate tofu lasagna for dinner and were served tofu cake for dessert. The residents of the commune, while claiming adherence to a new faith unlike any known system, were all clad in the typical orange flowing garments associated with Hinduism and its offshoot cult god, Hare Krishna. Their mannerisms and methods tended toward Hinduism. When we asked them about the apparent dominance of the Hindu belief system, they became indignant and argumentative.

We chatted with one family who had previously attended a Southern Baptist church. They gloried in their newfound spiritual enlightenment, claiming that Christianity was good but not complete without being amalgamated with all the other world religions. It was obvious that the fusion of all belief systems resulted, in their opinion, with a religion that most resembled Hinduism. They were deceived beyond all comprehension.

After dinner, as the climax of our day, we were taken into an assembly room where adherents gathered regularly to express worship to their leader. We waited, along with them, in nervous anticipation for the arrival of this man. We had heard talk of him all day long but had not yet seen him. When the doors opened and he entered, the gathered crowd stood to its feet in thunderous applause. He walked to the front and sat cross-legged before his admirers, who chanted and expressed devotion to him as if he were divine—in fact, they believed he was. One young girl, probably about fifteen or sixteen years of age, asked permission to approach him. She knelt down before him and proudly read a poem she had composed as an act of worship. Again, my heart broke as this sweet young girl heaped praise upon a mere man. The spiritual climate in that room was heavy and oppressive.

Forces of evil permeated that compound. I had the distinct impression that the gates of hell had been opened and I had walked into the sulfurous den of the devil himself. Although Christianity was purportedly in the mix, Jesus Christ had not been invited.

When we boarded our buses to return home, we sat in stunned and disgusted silence. Our hearts ached and our minds were numb. Like soldiers straggling and limping out of the battle, shell-shocked and dazed, we slowly regathered our senses. One missionary toward the rear of the bus began to sing softly a chorus of praise to Jesus. Before long, the entire bus was full of the melody of our worship. The peace and joy of Jesus began to push aside the darkness of the last few hours.

Part of our frustration came from the fact that our leaders instructed us that we were to be observers only. We could ask questions, but were not permitted to debate or to present our views. We were their guests and were told to respect their right to believe the way they wished. The day was so difficult because our voice had been silenced, even though voluntarily. Confronted with the errors and deception of the Lotus Community, our minds raced and our hearts yearned to tell them the good news of a real Savior, who had died for their sins. Unable to articulate our faith in Jesus, we grew sullen and mournful. Only when we rediscovered our voice and renewed our praise did joy again inundate our lives.

The Lotus Community is but a cross section of our world. What the people believed there, the world accepts as truth. The belief that there are many paths to God is growing in popularity.

The apostle Paul found such a belief system in Athens. Not wanting to offend any so-called god or goddess, the Athenians had filled their city with idols. They even had "an altar with this inscription, 'To an Unknown God'" (Acts 17:23). With no one way better than the others, all had to be appeased. Paul confronted their tolerance for all faiths by presenting to them the one and only way to God through Jesus Christ. Paul stood that day in the Areopagus of Athens and proclaimed the resurrection of Christ from the dead. By His death and resurrection, Jesus has provided access to God. We who follow Jesus understand that the resurrection gives undeniable proof of the veracity of the gospel. We declare unashamedly that Jesus is the only way to God.

The unbelieving world rejects the exclusive claims of Christianity. Satan continues to deceive individuals and people groups into denying Jesus Christ and accepting erroneous belief systems. Even in "Christian" America, Mormonism, a cult, and Islam, a world religion, are growing faster and seeing greater numbers of converts than is Christianity. Many more minor movements are attracting much attention as well. Some of Hollywood's superstars claim adherence to Scientology and Zen Buddhism. Some professional athletes have changed their names to identify with an Islamic influence in their lives. New Age beliefs that range from the occult to eastern religions often are a mixture of many different religious systems. Some, like pop star Madonna, claim to be "spiritual." Of course, to her spirituality means only an intense interest in spiritual things regardless of what those spiritual things might be. To us, it means devotion and commitment to Jesus Christ. To Madonna and the rest of the syncretistic world, "spiritual" often includes gurus, mediums, and psychics among other things.

It is popular today for a person to intermingle what he considers the best part of each religious system into a personalized way of life and thought. One may choose the meditation of yoga, the inwardness of Buddhism, the Karma of Hinduism, the brotherhood of Christianity, the separation of spirit and matter of animism, the belief in aliens of the New Agers, shake them all together and call it faith. It is, however, nothing more than spiritual darkness and confusion. This is not a new phenomenon. In the 1960s, fans of the Beatles thought the fabulous four were believers in Jesus, until the background words of "My Sweet Lord" were discovered. The song, in reality, was fashioned as praise to Krishna.

Believers in Jesus are increasingly at odds with a world that demands tolerance. The world discounts us as close-minded and bigoted because of our firm belief in Jesus Christ as *the* only way of salvation. Opposition is growing toward Christians and their message of a "narrow gate" leading to salvation and eternal life. The world declares that God has many faces and many voices. One may achieve, so the world thinks, eternal peace just as easily through transcendental meditation or the cycles of reincarnation as it can through faith in Jesus Christ. Not only are we criticized for our narrow-mindedness regarding the way of salvation, but we are also ridiculed for continuing to believe in the concept of hell. Even some who claim allegiance to Christ no longer hold an orthodox view of hell. Many of these nominal believers opt for some form of annihilationism (the belief that no one will experience the horrors of hell since God will simply cause their souls to cease to exist) or universalism (the belief that in the end, God will allow all people into heaven irrespective of their commitment to or faith in Him). A form of universalism is embraced by some postmodern church leaders under the title of "inclusivism" which keeps "the door open that others could be saved through Christ even if they never identified as Christians."[9] The disturbing question arising from this idea is: How can someone "be saved through Christ" without identifying with Him or His people? This door opens up to some form of the belief that all religions lead to God—a dangerous heresy.

The implication of this religious trend is that the Christian's voice becomes just one among many. There are so many voices vying for airtime that there is a real danger that our voices will be overwhelmed and silenced. One example of this danger is seen in a thirty-second commercial run by the Mormons that comes across as positive, upbeat, encouraging, and centered upon family values. They even offer a free copy of the King James Version of the Holy Bible. If you call that 800 number, you will not only receive the free Bible but also the Book of Mormon and other pieces of literature promoting their heretical beliefs.

Our church offers a Halloween alternative each year. Last year, a church member brought a young mother to talk with me in the midst of a very noisy and busy parking lot set up with games and carnival-type booths. The loud speaker blared with the names of youngsters who had won door prizes. Music from the cakewalk echoed from across the way. The young woman shared with me how she had been attending services at a local Kingdom Hall. She had some questions about the belief system of the Jehovah's Witnesses. In my excitement of sharing my faith with her, and in part because I had just finished a conversation with a church member about Mormonism, I began to tell her about the erroneous beliefs of the Mormons rather than the Jehovah's Witnesses. No wonder she looked at me with a bewildered expression. I asked her if she had a Bible and since she did not, I ran into the church building to grab one for her. Once inside, where quiet reigned, I realized with deep regret that I had given her the wrong information. When I handed the Bible to her, I apologized and shared very briefly the answers she was initially hoping to find for her questions. The moment was missed, though. Her children were anxious to get back to the games, and she had received information that resulted in more confusion, not less. I encouraged her to read the Bible I had given her as she walked away. Later that night, I asked God to forgive my blunder and to help her find the truth.

Toward the end of this year's Fall Festival, as I was walking around meeting people, a young woman with a warm smile came up to me and asked me if I remembered her. I did. She was the woman from the previous year. Again, I apologized to her, but she stopped me in mid sentence. With a smile on her face, she told me that she had quit going to the Kingdom Hall not long after our conversation. She began attending another church in the area and had recently received Christ as her personal Savior and Lord. I rejoiced with her and quietly thanked God that He was able to reach her in spite of my ineptitude. In a spiritual arena filled with many voices, we must somehow make our voice heard. We must speak up for Jesus Christ and speak loudly enough and often enough that people hear our voices. We cannot allow the voice of truth to be drowned out by the many voices of alternative religious systems. The devil has disguised his voice, masquerading as an "angel of light" (2 Corinthians 11:14). If our voices do not offer a clarion call for Jesus, our message of hope and forgiveness will be ignored.

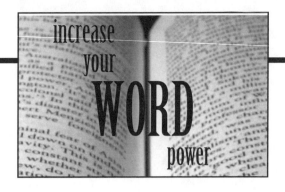

1   If you do not already have John 3:16 memorized, commit it to memory now. Think about how this verse refers to Jesus: He is God's only begotten Son. What does this verse say about the uniqueness of Jesus? About the uniqueness of the salvation provided through Jesus?

2   Do you know someone who is an adherent of another religious system? Begin a conversation with them by asking them what they believe about Jesus. You may receive some interesting answers. Thank them for sharing with you. At home, think about their answers and try to find Bible passages that might help illuminate their thinking about Jesus. On another occasion, ask them if you can share what you believe about Jesus. This might open a door for a wonderful witnessing conversation.

CHAPTER SIX

SPEAK WITH A GOSPEL ACCENT

The best compliment I ever received while attempting to speak French came from a photographer to whom we had taken our sons. After briefly talking about the types of portraits we wanted, he asked, "Are you German?" I was stunned. Usually it is so obvious when an American speaks French. "Bonjour, ya'll," sticks out like a sore thumb. That he thought I was European was to me a great achievement. Not long after, however, as I waited for a train, two college students approached and asked me if I knew the time. When I asked them to repeat the question, they looked at each other, laughed, and turned to find somebody smarter. Again, I was stunned. They knew I was a foreigner, and probably an American, from just that one word response to their question. Even though I learned French fairly well, my accent always gave me away. French ears, finely tuned to the symphony of their language, recoiled as I hit every sour note possible.

Do the people we encounter every day recognize us quickly as Christians? How many words must we speak before our listeners surmise that we belong to Jesus? What an embarrassment when a friend of several months exclaims in surprise, "I didn't know you were a Christian!"

We need to learn to speak with a gospel accent. Have you

noticed that we will talk about anything and everything except that which matters most—faith in Jesus Christ? In 1992, I was a leader for a student witnessing team at the Winter Olympics in Albertville, France. We had opportunities to witness to the many tourists and spectators who had traveled to this most beautiful location in the French Alps. We had gospel tracts in several different languages. Of course, many Americans were present. I enjoyed meeting and speaking to many of them, but I will remember one man particularly. He was a big, burly guy and when we began to talk about spiritual matters he stopped us cold, saying, "I decided before I came that there were two things I would not talk about over here: politics and religion." I do not know where this man was in his spiritual pilgrimage; he would not let me find out. It seems to me though that he typifies many Christians today who have made a prior decision not to talk about spiritual things.

Speaking with a gospel accent means letting our speech be seasoned through and through with the words and attitudes of our Lord. Before we address this issue as it relates to our witness to unbelievers, we must confess that even among believers, even at church, we talk very little of Jesus. I think I first noticed this at seminary. Students who had given their lives to Christian ministry and who were in the process of preparing for their life's work seldom spoke of the Lord in conversations with one another. Baseball, yes. Stock market, yes. Research papers, yes. Jesus, seldom!

During my seminary pastorate, I discovered the same reticence to bring Jesus into our conversations. We would complain about the Dallas Cowboys, but we would not even whisper about Jesus, that is, until the worship hour began. During that high and holy moment, we sang about Him, talked about Him, prayed to Him, and called people to believe in Him. But when the service was over, we tucked Him away behind the scenes. We can turn on and turn off Jesus like clockwork. Eleven o'clock on Sunday, Jesus on. Noon, Jesus off.

If we are ashamed to speak to one another about Jesus, then no wonder we do not speak to the lost about Him. Is it any wonder that unbelievers do not know much about the Lord? They simply do not hear anyone talking about Him. They do not attend church, they do not read the Bible, they do not listen to Christian radio or watch Christian television, they do not pay attention to church signs that sloganeer the Christian faith. One of the biggest churches in the nation sits on over eighty acres of land at a prominent intersection in its city. Recently, a community survey revealed that many in the city had no idea the church even existed. Its building is easily the most identifiable piece of architecture in the immediate area. Lost people just are not paying attention to the things we think draw them to the Savior. We think that a wonderful building and a conspicuous sign will draw people in. If they are not noticing these things, then how can they know anything at all about Jesus? The simple answer is that we must speak with a gospel accent; we must speak Jesus into their world.

I am not talking about presenting the gospel at this point (that may do little good if they know nothing of Jesus). I am talking about simply letting Jesus into our conversations. We claim that

He is the most important aspect of our lives—the very center of our existence—yet we do not talk about Him. Gandhi, a dedicated Hindu, quoted Jesus more often than we do.

Maybe we do not speak of Jesus because we really do not know Him very well and are simply unfamiliar with His teachings. Maybe we are simply embarrassed by what He stands for, somehow thinking His teachings are out of date. The apostle Peter struggled with this problem. Incidentally, it was his accent that gave him away. Jesus had warned Peter of his impending denials, but Peter ran off into the night when the soldiers came to arrest Jesus. He doubled back and followed Jesus, along with John, into the courtyard of the High Priest. There he would not dare risk anyone identifying him as a follower of Jesus. When confronted by the gatekeeper (a servant girl) and by others warming themselves by the fire, Peter denied knowing Jesus. With each denial, he became a bit more tense, even swearing in a vain attempt to disassociate himself from Jesus. His third and final denial had to be forceful and emphatic, for those standing near him pressed the issue: "Surely you are one of them, for your accent gives you away" (Matthew 26:73 NIV). Betrayed by the tones and intonations of his voice, Peter cursed and swore, "I don't know the man!" (v. 74 NIV). He could not bring himself to say His name but detachedly referred to Him as if a total stranger.

One way or another, our accent will give us away. Our silence as to spiritual matters will betray our faithlessness. So, too, our conversations about our Lord testify to a living and unashamed faith. Speaking with a gospel accent involves

Christlike attitudes. When we defend some conviction, proclaim some ethical truth, or stand against some injustice, we bring Jesus' teachings to bear upon the issue at hand. Of course, someone could defend the same conviction, tout the same ethical truth, and stand against injustice without having a personal commitment to Jesus Christ. When we take our stand for the truth, we must make it clear that we are standing for *The Truth* (see John 14:6). If not, we may be seen as a good and moral person, but not necessarily as a Christian person. This is exactly why we must speak often of Jesus and base our convictions upon His Word.

Recently, I filled my shopping cart with everything on the list my wife gave me. I piled it in, taking extra care not to crush the delicate objects like eggs and bread. I paid for my groceries using the self-service lane and headed for my car. As I was unloading the cart, I noticed a small tube of lip balm that was not in a sack. I double checked the receipt and realized that I had not paid for this item. After emptying the cart, I locked the car and headed back inside. I found the cashier overseeing the self-service lanes and explained my situation. She looked at me as if she had never seen an honest person before. My response to her "thank you so very much" was simple and to the point: "It's because of Jesus that I returned to pay for the item." I wanted her to know that I was not acting in such a way because I was a good person but because I have a value system based upon my faith in Jesus Christ. In this simple yet profound way, I brought Jesus into my conversation and pointed to Him as the reason for my actions. My speech reflected my Christlike attitude of honesty, but I took no credit for the good that I did. It is all about Jesus and our conversations ought to reflect this truth.

Again, speaking with a gospel accent involves Christlike speech patterns. It is so very easy to adopt the speech patterns of the world around us. Explicatives abound and in the heat of the moment, if we are not keeping watch over our thoughts and mouths, we can let loose with words that would certainly displease our Lord. Furthermore, consider how easy it is to allow unbelievers with whom we work or associate to set the tone and tenor of our conversations. We timidly adopt their content because it is less threatening than pushing a conversation toward spiritual matters.

In all of the witnessing encounters I have had over the years, the hardest part of the conversation is to turn it toward Jesus. Once I have successfully turned the conversation toward the Lord, I have no problem presenting the simple truths that comprise a gospel presentation. My struggle is getting started. I confess that sometimes I have just let the discussion of mundane and ordinary things continue on until the visit is over, never broaching the subject of spiritual need. It is just easier to talk about anything other than Jesus. In my mind, I have justified such failed witnessing attempts as relationship building. But such justification is a veiled attempt to make me feel better about my lack of boldness in witness. Shame on me! Why do we allow ourselves to be intimidated and to become weak-kneed when it comes to speaking of Jesus? We need to develop a habit of speaking often of Jesus and His Word.

Speaking with a gospel accent involves using Christlike

words—no, more than that—Christ's words. Why do we not speak the words that Jesus spoke? They are, in fact, the greatest words ever spoken. Now we would not want to speak arrogantly as if we were Jesus himself, but why can we not bring Jesus into the conversation by applying His teachings to the subject matter we are discussing with others? We can do this by direct quote or by summary of what Jesus has said. Speaking with a gospel accent might very well mean entering a discussion with words such as "You know, Jesus said something about this issue . . ."

Your response to this might be "If I talk like that, everybody will think I am a fanatic!" Indeed, they might, but our world could use a few more Christ-fanatics. We will yell and scream at the top of our lungs when our favorite athletes do well in a game. We will quote the ramblings of charged-up sportscasters and prognosticators. We will debate the pros and cons of players and teams, but we dare not present ourselves as passionate about our faith. Maybe our world would begin to take note of our message if we would get excited about it ourselves. Jesus does have something to say about any and every issue we may discuss with others, but we act as if He does not. We leave Him out of our conversations as if He were some uninformed sports-fan-wanna-be who knows nothing of which He talks. Jesus' words are the truest words ever spoken and we must bring them into our daily deliberations.

Let us think about the apostle Peter for a moment more. This one who gave himself away by his accent in the High Priest's courtyard was later again identified with Jesus by his manner of speech. This time, however, he was not shrinking away from would-be opponents. He was standing his ground against the authority of the religious elite of the day. After having healed the beggar outside the Beautiful Gate of the Temple in Jerusalem, Peter and John were taken into custody for questioning. The prior Peter would have denied being present when the miracle took place, but this renewed version of Peter stood toe-to-toe with his accusers and they could not shake him into denial. Luke records, "Now as they observed the confidence of Peter and John, and understood that they were uneducated and untrained men, they were amazed, and began to recognize them as having been with Jesus" (Acts 4:13).

Our great need is not more sophistication, more education, or more training, but more dependence upon God's Spirit who calls us to be witnesses. What we need is to open our mouths and speak. We must quit hiding our identity by disguising our accent. We must let the world know we are followers of Jesus by our accent and by the manner in which we talk.

Teyah is probably the cutest little girl I have ever known. Her parents adopted her from China when she was just a few years old. She came to America not knowing anything except a Chinese orphanage and the Chinese language. Of course, upon her arrival she was immersed into our American culture and language. During worship, she would join the other children who came to sit at my feet for the children's message. At first, she did not understand a word that I said, but slowly she realized that I was speaking about God. Her parents taught her about Jesus at home. Not long after she began to say some English words and phrases, tragedy struck her extended family. When I heard the

Woody D. Wilson

news, I raced to the home to offer comfort and to pray with the family. After knocking on the door, I stepped into the family room. The first person to see me was Teyah. Surely, she did not comprehend the events that were swirling around her. When she saw me, however, she immediately brightened and to my surprise she exclaimed, "Jesus!" and ran to hug me around my leg. What a humbling experience. Somehow, lost in translation, she had identified me with Jesus, but then, no, she was right—in some form that day I was Jesus to her hurting family. She had gleaned from the children's messages on Sundays that I was speaking for Jesus, and that by my words I represented Him. I shall ever be moved by her childlike response of faith that sad day. In my weak and unsteady way, I had somehow spoken to her with a gospel accent.

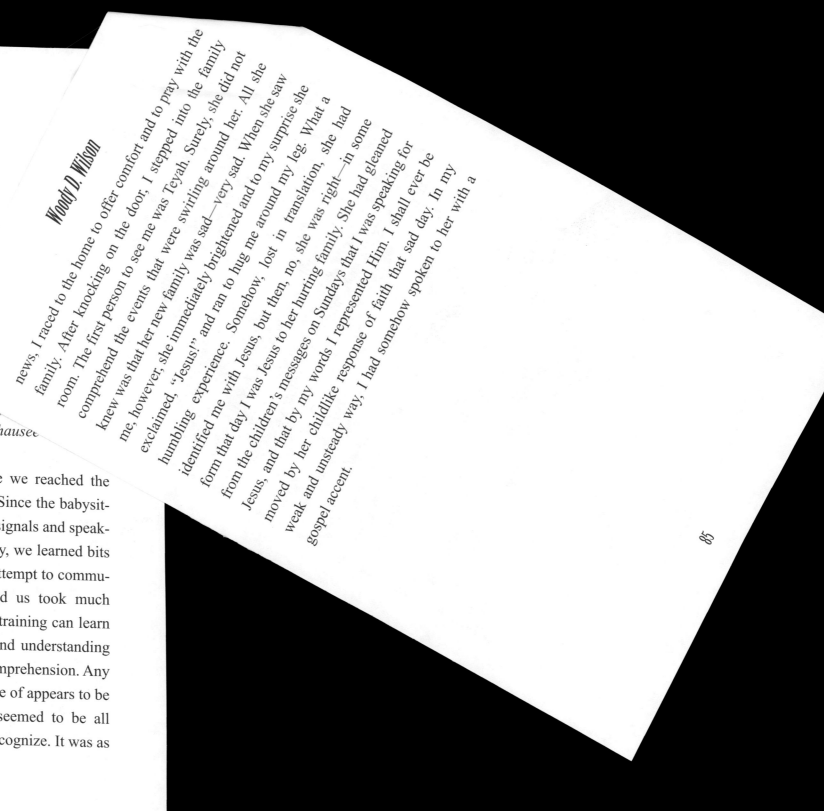

CHAPTER SEVEN

HE WHO HAS EARS TO

While my wife and I attended lan[...] France, we lived on the thirteenth f[...] apartment building. There were two[...] numbered floors and one for the [...] included riding down to the ninth floor to dr[...] at the babysitter, then riding to the *rez de chausee[...]* floor.

Our language learning began long before we reached the institute where our formal classes took place. Since the babysitter knew no English, we first resorted to hand signals and speaking English a bit louder than normal. Gradually, we learned bits and pieces of her language and could at least attempt to communicate verbally. Understanding what she told us took much longer. A person who has very little language training can learn to speak some basic phrases, while hearing and understanding another language requires a more advanced comprehension. Any language you do not have a working knowledge of appears to be spoken very quickly. Syllables and sounds seemed to be all mixed up as we listened for words we might recognize. It was as if we were wearing earmuffs.

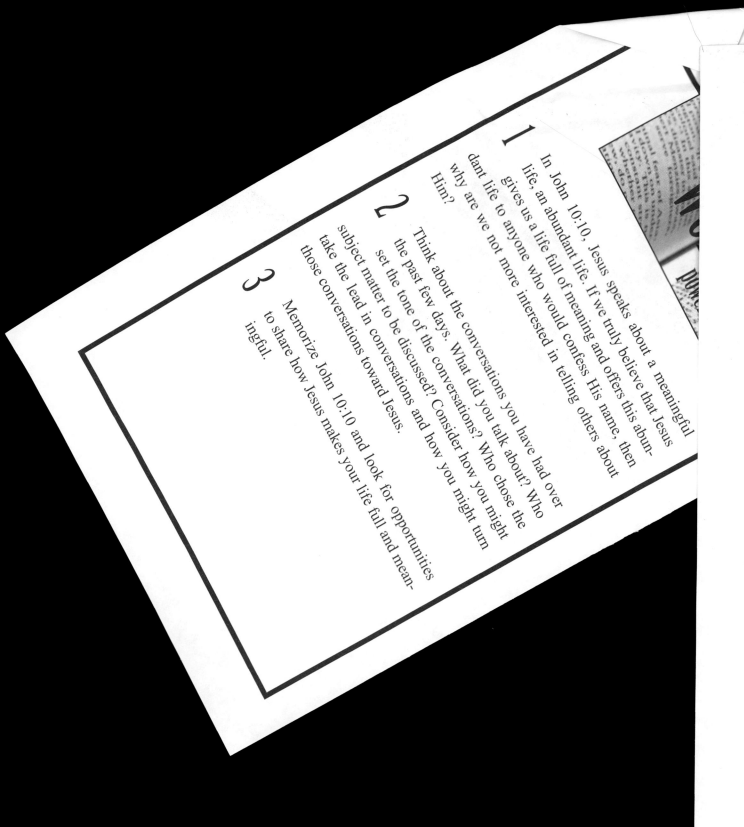

1 In John 10:10, Jesus speaks about a meaningful life, an abundant life. If we truly believe that Jesus gives us a life full of meaning and offers this abundant life to anyone who would confess His name, then why are we not more interested in telling others about Him?

2 Think about the conversations you have had over the past few days. What did you talk about? Who set the tone of the conversations? Who chose the subject matter to be discussed? Consider how you might take the lead in conversations and how you might turn those conversations toward Jesus.

3 Memorize John 10:10 and look for opportunities to share how Jesus makes your life full and meaningful.

The Shadow of Babel

The second stage of our descent each morning brought unique challenges. Our babysitter knew we did not understand and so attempted little conversation, but the strangers on the elevator assumed, at least at first, that we spoke their language. While we found the people of France to be very friendly and patient with our language gaffs, the elevator was a daily humbling experience. Initially, before I had any ability with the language, when someone spoke to me on the elevator, I would answer with a polite yet uninformed *oui* (the French word for yes pronounced 'wee'). If my interlocutor persisted in conversing with me, I often countered by adding another *oui* or two to my response, even though I had no clue as to what was said or asked.

You are familiar with the little game parents play with the bare toes of their children—"this little piggy went to market, this little piggy stayed home. . . ." Well, I was the little missionary who went "oui, oui, oui, all the way down." Who knows what I agreed to or how ignorant I must have appeared. Months later, when we became more proficient in conversation, these same elevator mates never once referred back to those awkward moments of our not being able to understand. They became some of our biggest fans as we grew in the knowledge and practice of their language.

Before we can effectively communicate the gospel of Jesus Christ, we must become good listeners. We tend to be so wrapped up in our own problems and the details of our own lives that we rarely listen to what others are saying. Sometimes when I am in a group of people, I will step out of the conversation to observe what is transpiring. More often than not each person takes his or her turn at offering a soliloquy. The other grunt something that appears to be supportive, but in re are just biding their time until it is their turn.

Shamefully, we approach our witnessing in much the same way. We know what we want to say (because we have been trained to say it that way), but we give little attention to the one to whom we are saying it. We will have our say regardless of the hurt or need of the person before us and regardless of what the person may want to say to us. I have noticed in my own scheduled witnessing encounters that it does me little good to plan what I am going to say. If I map out the conversation, the one to whom I am speaking will ask a question or make a statement that necessitates a different approach. Seldom does the conversation follow my predetermined path. I have learned to listen first, both to the person with whom I am engaged in conversation and to the Holy Spirit.

A church sign read: "Jesus is the answer! Now what was your question?" Ultimately, a truer statement could not be made, but the challenge of our witness is to show each person how Jesus answers their particular question or meets their personal problem. We must not write them off with generic slogans or canned presentations. We ought to take the time to listen and apply the gospel to their lives and problems.

But, Ah, there's the rub—time! How wonderful and miraculous it would have been if, when our plane landed on French soil, we would have automatically known the language of the French people. Of course, that did not happen. When our plane landed, all I could think of was the Spanish words I had learned in high school. I knew English would not work, so my mind ran to alternative words. Learning French took time, much time, a lifetime. Most career missionaries freely admit that even after many years they are still in the process of learning the language in which they minister and witness. If you were honest, you would say that you are still learning English (and it is your heart language).

Most witnessing efforts necessitate that we take the time to build a relationship with the lost person and that we truly listen to their needs. This requires a time commitment to an individual or a family. Enough of our "hit and run" attempts at winning the lost. We go in "guns blazing" and get a decision at the expense of the soul. Many seekers and interested people are "lost" to the church because we have besieged their homes with rapid-fire, automatic-weapon type witnessing. It is as if we are saying, "I have some great news to share with you. You have approximately 5-10 minutes to hear it, understand it, appreciate it, and receive it. Ready? Here are four simple truths you must know." We zip through our presentation and call for a decision—a life-altering, lifetime commitment to something they have just heard about, maybe for the first time. When my wife reads a novel, she likes to tell me the story as she goes. Not too long ago she was reading *The Wishing Star* by Marian Wells.[10] I have never read the story myself, but my wife enjoyed it. As she relayed the story line to me, she told me about a young woman named Jenny. When confronted with a decision about which she had little information, Jenny said she had never heard of being asked to believe something she knew nothing about. Is this not what we often expect when we witness to many unbelievers, especially in this postmodern era? We expect them to put away their personal belief systems and embrace a Christian worldview after giving them only a brief sketch of Christ's teachings.

I fear that much of our witnessing efforts are nothing more than face-to-face telemarketing schemes. We talk fast, do not listen, and pressure the person to buy into what we are selling. Once while I was exercising in my garage, two insurance salesmen stopped by unannounced. Just the day before, my wife and I had been wondering how we were going to obtain health insurance for our diabetic son. I mentioned this need to the two men, who replied promptly that their company could meet that need. With that assurance, I invited them into my home to let them tell me about their various plans. Within minutes, I realized that they had simply used my son's condition as a way to get a foot in the door. In fact, they had no such coverage for a teenage diabetic. Once inside, though, they gave me their hard sell. Frustrated by their overly aggressive and empty promises, I turned them away as quickly as I could. Unfortunately, what happened to me is what happens to many church prospects to whom we make evangelistic visits. We want to get to our selling point and fail to listen or to give them time and space to digest what we are saying.

On occasion, I have overseen this process of "losing" someone to the cause of Christ. On the surface, it appeared that such a person was saved. I am convinced, however, that his "Yes, I will pray that prayer" masked what he was really thinking: "I'll do anything to get you out of my home." Tragically, this is the result of speaking the gospel without first listening to the need or problem in the person's life.

The Shadow of Babel

Mike was a young man whose life had been miraculously spared. He fell asleep at the wheel of his pickup truck early one morning as he was driving toward his favorite fishing spot. He drove off the road and hit a tree. The boat he was towing sliced through the cab of the truck and out through the windshield. Mike sustained numerous life-threatening injuries. He was flown to a trauma center for treatment. Upon closer examination, the doctors discovered that his aorta had been cut in the accident. He should have bled out in a matter of minutes at the scene of the accident. Without medical explanation, the injury clotted, giving surgeons time to repair it. Mike acknowledges that God spared his life. I visited him in the hospital and the church prayed earnestly for his recovery. Several months prior to his accident, he and his wife had given birth to twin girls. He rejoiced that God allowed him to live to see his daughters grow up. Through it all, Mike did not attend church services, although he kept promising me he would.

That autumn, our church began an intensive evangelism training that required the memorization of a short gospel presentation. Team leaders were to model the presentation week by week to their team members as they gradually learned the material. On the first night of visits, I took my team to Mike's home. His giggling twin girls who had on no clothes greeted us at the door. They were getting ready for their bath. Mike's wife led the girls out of the front room where my team and Mike were seated. As the conversation progressed toward the gospel presentation, the girls finished their bath and ran back into the room, still naked. Mom wrapped a towel around one, dressed the other, and news, I raced to the home to offer comfort and to pray with the family. After knocking on the door, I stepped into the family room. The first person to see me was Teyah. Surely, she did not comprehend the events that were swirling around her. All she knew was that her new family was sad—very sad. When she saw me, however, she immediately brightened and to my surprise she exclaimed, "Jesus!" and ran to hug me around my leg. What a humbling experience. Somehow, lost in translation, she had identified me with Jesus, but then, no, she was right—in some form that day I was Jesus to her hurting family. She had gleaned from the children's messages on Sundays that I was speaking for Jesus, and that by my words I represented Him. I shall ever be moved by her childlike response of faith that sad day. In my weak and unsteady way, I had somehow spoken to her with a gospel accent.

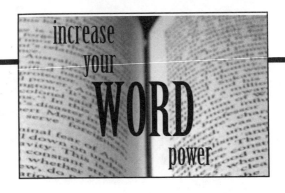

increase your **WORD** power

1   In John 10:10, Jesus speaks about a meaningful life, an abundant life. If we truly believe that Jesus gives us a life full of meaning and offers this abundant life to anyone who would confess His name, then why are we not more interested in telling others about Him?

2   Think about the conversations you have had over the past few days. What did you talk about? Who set the tone of the conversations? Who chose the subject matter to be discussed? Consider how you might take the lead in conversations and how you might turn those conversations toward Jesus.

3   Memorize John 10:10 and look for opportunities to share how Jesus makes your life full and meaningful.

CHAPTER SEVEN

HE WHO HAS EARS TO HEAR

While my wife and I attended language school in Tours, France, we lived on the thirteenth floor of an eighteen-story apartment building. There were two elevators, one for the even numbered floors and one for the odd. Our morning routine included riding down to the ninth floor to drop off our children at the babysitter, then riding to the *rez de chausee* or ground floor.

Our language learning began long before we reached the institute where our formal classes took place. Since the babysitter knew no English, we first resorted to hand signals and speaking English a bit louder than normal. Gradually, we learned bits and pieces of her language and could at least attempt to communicate verbally. Understanding what she told us took much longer. A person who has very little language training can learn to speak some basic phrases, while hearing and understanding another language requires a more advanced comprehension. Any language you do not have a working knowledge of appears to be spoken very quickly. Syllables and sounds seemed to be all mixed up as we listened for words we might recognize. It was as if we were wearing earmuffs.

The Shadow of Babel

The second stage of our descent each morning brought unique challenges. Our babysitter knew we did not understand and so attempted little conversation, but the strangers on the elevator assumed, at least at first, that we spoke their language. While we found the people of France to be very friendly and patient with our language gaffs, the elevator was a daily humbling experience. Initially, before I had any ability with the language, when someone spoke to me on the elevator, I would answer with a polite yet uninformed *oui* (the French word for yes pronounced 'wee'). If my interlocutor persisted in conversing with me, I often countered by adding another *oui* or two to my response, even though I had no clue as to what was said or asked.

You are familiar with the little game parents play with the bare toes of their children—"this little piggy went to market, this little piggy stayed home. . . ." Well, I was the little missionary who went "oui, oui, oui, all the way down." Who knows what I agreed to or how ignorant I must have appeared. Months later, when we became more proficient in conversation, these same elevator mates never once referred back to those awkward moments of our not being able to understand. They became some of our biggest fans as we grew in the knowledge and practice of their language.

Before we can effectively communicate the gospel of Jesus Christ, we must become good listeners. We tend to be so wrapped up in our own problems and the details of our own lives that we rarely listen to what others are saying. Sometimes when I am in a group of people, I will step out of the conversation to observe what is transpiring. More often than not each person disappeared into the back of the house. Since my responsibility as a team leader was to model the presentation, I did just that. Through distraction after distraction, I pressed on and pressed Mike for a decision. He seemed responsive and agreed to pray the sinner's prayer. We rejoiced with him, prayed for him again, and departed with words of encouragement, stressing how important it was for him to be in church on Sunday. Nevertheless, he did not attend that next Sunday, nor has he attended since that night.

Back at the church after that visit, we shared our joyous news with the other teams who had reassembled after their visits. We had successfully shared the gospel! Or had we? To be honest— No, we had not. Emphatically, no! We failed to listen and to be sensitive to the needs in their home. How much better would it have been to share the gospel with both husband and wife togeth- er after the daughters had been tucked neatly into bed? In that setting, we could have listened, answered questions, and gently pointed them to the Savior. Why didn't we? For one thing, it did not fit our schedule. The twins' bedtime was eight o'clock, but our team needed to be back at the church by 7:45 P.M. It would have disrupted our evangelism training schedule to do it right. Perhaps several visits would have been necessary to help them understand Christ's claim upon their lives. We would rather give the ten-minute version because it is simpler for us.

What is the goal of evangelism? Is it to make us feel better about ourselves because we have shared the gospel? Or rather, is it to draw lost people to the Savior? To this day, I regret pressing Mike without any thought of the situation in his home that night.

Incidentally, about a year later, Mike's wife and children began attending church services. One Sunday, one of the girls wandered from her seat, came up on the platform, and sat on my lap for a few minutes. I wondered then, even as I wonder now years later, what a difference there would be in this family's life if I had listened to the need of the hour rather than press Mike for a nominal decision.

Now do not run out and cancel all your evangelism training sessions. God can and does use them. You may have gotten the idea that I am opposed to any memorized presentation of the gospel. Of course, I am not. Alvin Reid sums up my thoughts on the matter: "Some people criticize memorized presentations because they are 'canned.' In my experience, *any* presentation of the gospel—a marked New Testament, tract, or testimony—is canned, if the person sharing Christ doesn't care about the person hearing the message."[11] All that I am asking is that you take time to listen, to hear, and then to respond with the gospel that meets the person right where they are. Jesus often said, "He who has an ear, let him hear." As you listen to what God says, may you also learn to listen to what the lost are saying. It will make you a much more effective witness.

It is important to add at this point a further comment from Alvin Reid. Following the above quote, he adds, "But the discipline such an approach (i.e., a memorized gospel presentation) offers has aided many believers in their growth in personal evangelism."[12] These comments are written in his chapter, "The Need of the Hour: Personal Evangelism." He began this chapter by saying, "It is obvious that most Americans are better at talking about evangelism than actually doing it."[13] In the midst of this chapter, he presents the CWT (Continuing Witnessing Training) model as an effective tool for personal evangelism. This training, in fact, helped me greatly. While I was still quite shy early in my ministry, I went through the CWT process. It helped me verbalize the gospel during a time when I had a hard time verbalizing anything. As a missionary, I again studied through the CWT material in the French language. The profit was great, for it gave me the words I needed to witness across the language barrier that I faced daily. I did not have to search for words; I had put them in my mind and heart.

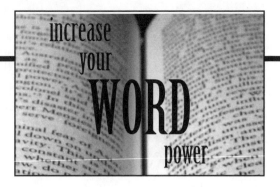

increase your WORD power

1   James 1:22 says, "But prove yourselves doers of the Word, and not merely hearers who delude themselves." Think about this comment of Alvin Reid: "It is obvious that most Americans are better at talking about evangelism than actually doing it." Do you amen your pastor when he speaks about witnessing or missions but fail to involve yourself in these activities? Do you always think about witnessing in terms of what someone else should be doing?

2   Read the story of the Woman at the Well in John 4. Notice that Jesus met her where she was in life and addressed her perceived needs. Notice also that He answered her questions and responded to her doubts. Jesus even used her evasive tactics to lead her to a deeper level of understanding. He led her from where she was to where she needed to be. The woman, in turn, believed and became a bold witness to the people of her city.

3   Is there someone at work or some acquaintance that you have not been listening to? What steps could you take to insure that you become a better listener? After listening, how could you present the gospel in such a way that it would meet the person's needs?

Write three steps in the spaces below:

1) _____

2) _____

3) _____

CHAPTER EIGHT

COMMON GROUND, HOLY GROUND

The old man must have been overwhelmed. I was. Opening
ceremonies of the 1992 Winter Olympics was just an hour away.
The streets of Albertville, France, were overrun with pedestrians
moving toward the stadium where the lighting of the Olympic
torch would signal the commencement of the Games. The night
before, I stood alongside a cobblestone street and watched the
Olympic flame come into town on its final leg of a long journey
from Greece. I snapped a quick photo or two, and then hoisted a
friend on my shoulders so she could see.

I am almost positive the old French man did not understand
all the activity. He seemed oblivious to the flood of people passing in front of him as he sat on a park bench—his park bench—
and stared blankly at the snow-capped mountains that loomed
just ahead. He must have wondered why the world had besieged
his city. At least he had his park bench. I imagine he sat there
every day, sometimes talking with a friend, sometimes watching
a game of *boules*, sometimes so deep in thought that he was not
conscious of the existence of any other soul. I met him on just
such a day. He barely noticed that I had sat down beside him.

My assigned task for the afternoon had been to stop and talk
to as many people as possible as they made their way to the sta-

dium. Impossible! They would not stop and did not want to talk. After a while, I stopped trying. A half an hour earlier, the crush had separated me from my colleagues. I wandered a bit aimlessly yet in the general direction of the stadium. I did not have a ticket, so I soaked in the festive atmosphere. This was a world-class event! My wanderings brought me, pushed and bumped and somewhat bruised, to a clearing in the midst of the rivers of excited sports enthusiasts, converging on a temporary stadium where history would be made, dreams would be fulfilled, while others would be shattered by disappointment. The sun was just beginning to hide behind the tallest mountain peek; shadows lengthened as day turned to dusk; an old man lost in thought and heartbreak welcomed me to his bench. I was tired and sat in silence as I caught my breath and watched the faceless multitudes file past.

I turned slightly toward the man and noticed how hollow his eyes seemed and how furrowed was his brow. Was he bothered by the congestion of people, by my presence, or by something else much deeper? Wanting to begin a conversation that I could turn quickly to spiritual matters, I gestured toward the mountains and made some remark about how beautiful and majestic they were and how God was so good in giving as such awe-inspiring views. Without batting an eye, the old man refused to agree. His words seemed out of place in that setting. Perhaps he had seen the mountains so often that he did not really see them anymore. His words betrayed his heart. "I cannot believe in God," he said. It was the "cannot" that threw me. Most say, "Do not," or "Will not," but this weathered old man said "cannot."

There had to be a reason, so I asked politely, "Why can you not believe in God?" Again, his response caught me, "Because God allowed my son to die." He seemed eager to tell his brief story. He had probably rehearsed it hundreds of times. He told me how his only son had been tragically killed as a young man, leaving him all alone in the world. Since that day, he could not believe in a God who would allow such heartache. He had been in this condition now for nearly twenty years. Every day, he would sit on his park bench and curse the mountains as they silently testified to the God he despised. Bitterness can cause some very irrational emotions.

I retreated, leaning back on the bench, searching the shadowy mountaintops for a gospel response. The last of the spectators were running now to the gates of the stadium; few people remained in the streets. I sat in shared grief with a man I hardly knew. We drank in the approaching night and the coolness of the evening breeze. I leaned forward and offered the only comfort I could find. I do not know what the man thought of my words; he did not give a verbal reply. His eyes, however, darted to meet mine for the first time during our conversation as if he recognized a voice he had not heard for many years. I trust that it was the voice of God spoken through me. Sometimes God gives us wisdom beyond our years and words that hit the mark. This was one of those times. All I said was this: "You know, God understands how hurt you are, for He allowed His only son to die, too, and it broke His heart. Jesus died on a cruel cross in order to offer forgiveness for sins. I do not know why your son had to die, but I do know that God loves you." I witnessed what I believe was a silent reconnection with God that day. The death of a son was common ground between a man and the God who was pursuing him. As I walked away, after having bid the man farewell, I realized that I had been sitting on holy ground.

Witnessing transforms common ground into holy ground. Before we can help people connect with God in those most holy of moments, we must first connect with them on some shared level of interest and understanding, "finding common points of mutual identification that provide the basis for the transmission of shared meanings."[14] Sharing the gospel of Jesus Christ begins with the search for common ground—some point of recognition and connection, some way of identifying with a person. It is what W. Oscar Thompson, in his book *Concentric Circles of Concern*, called "building bridges." In a chapter by this title, Thompson discusses "utilizing points of contact"[15] to identify with the needs of people. These contact points may be times of joy, such as weddings, anniversaries, the birth of a baby, or a promotion at work, to name a few. Your point of contact may be during a time of stress and loss, such as a death or illness, loss of job, marital problems, or anything that may bring about disappointment and crisis. More often, a contact point may be just the normal activities of day-to-day living. Thompson affirms, "As you are building bridges, opportunities will open for you to share the gospel."[16]

The incarnation, Jesus' coming into the world as man, was God's search for common ground. God desired to connect with humanity and did so as Jesus took on flesh and bone, fully experiencing human life. Jesus identified with people in order to make a connection that could lead them to the holy ground of salvation. The Bible states, "We do not have a high priest who is unable to sympathize with our weaknesses, but we have one who has been tempted in every way, just as we are—yet was without sin. Let us then approach the throne of grace with confidence, so that we may receive mercy and find grace to help us in our time of need" (Hebrews 4:15-16 NIV).

Missionaries are taught to be incarnational in their approach to evangelism and ministry. Becoming one with and identifying with people makes our witness believable and authentic. If we see ourselves as better than and superior to those "poor sinners," a true connection will be impossible to achieve. During my time at language school in Tours, France, I met and became friends with a missionary doctor. He was a very bright young man on his way to West Africa to serve the physical and spiritual needs of the people there. One day, I accompanied him as he went to take care of some business. It did not go well, and he became very frustrated. As we walked away from that encounter, his anger boiled over as he let off steam to me. He stuck out his little finger and exclaimed about the Frenchman he had been dealing with, "I have more intelligence in my little finger than that man has in his entire brain!" Granted, he was upset, but I was bewildered by what he said. If that was his attitude about the French, would he have an equally arrogant attitude about the people God had called him to serve in West Africa?

If, on the other hand, we consider ourselves fellow strugglers and pilgrims, common ground has already been discovered. Because Jesus identified with us in our needs and hurts, we can identify with other hurting people at the point of their need. Paul exhorts us to "rejoice with those who rejoice, and weep with those who weep" (Romans 12:15). Personally, I find it easier to mourn with those who face sorrow than it is to rejoice with those whose happiness is overflowing. Opportunities for a witnessing connection are often deeper and more greatly appreciated when we stand with those who mourn.

We must also, even though it is more difficult, attempt to bring Jesus into the times of success and joy. When people are hurting, they sense a need for God, but when they are experiencing times of rejoicing, they often feel as if they can handle life on their own. God is not just a refuge for the hurting but also an intimate friend with whom we may share our times of celebration. He is a constant companion who walks along with us through the mundane and uneventful episodes of life as well as through the trying times that are full of danger or opportunity. His presence in our lives transforms every aspect of who we are. Likewise, our presence in the shared moments of mutual concern may very well transform the commonplace occurrences of life into a sacred encounter with the living God.

Sometimes God surprises us with the common ground we may establish with the lost and unchurched. I have learned that I can never out-plan or out-guess God's mysterious ways. In the days of my youth, baseball was the center of my life. I lived it and breathed it deeply. My dream was to play professional ball. It appeared that God had given me all the abilities necessary to make the dream come true. I had speed on the base paths, power at the plate, flawless glove work in the field, and a cannon for an arm. Pro scouts were contacting my high school coaches with interest. I had always planned to attend college and had several fine offers. Dallas Baptist University showed the most interest and I departed for Texas just five days after my high school graduation to play in their summer league. Homesickness set in and I struggled to adjust, but in my first three games, I had three hits and displayed my speed and arm strength. Then my world fell apart. All the things that came so naturally to me (when to slide, when to swing, how to judge a fly ball) suddenly left me. I was a power hitter who could not make contact, an impeccable fielder who could no longer catch a simple pop up. I was embarrassing myself on the field.

The day after a game in which I struck out four times, dropped two routine fly balls, and fell down running after another, I called the coach to inform him I was quitting. He thought that was a good idea and encouraged me to go home. The dream was shattered! I remained in Texas for several more weeks, living with my grandparents. My grandmother was a member of the Sagamore Hill Baptist Church. On Sunday mornings I sat with her in worship. The Sunday after my baseball career ended, I sat dejectedly in the pew and stewed in my juices. I had no plan for my future. The pastor, Fred Swank, best known for raising up dozens of young preachers, began his message with these words: "God has revealed to my heart that someone here this morning will surrender to preach." I slumped deeper into my padded seat, thinking that I did not even need to listen. I was not going to be a preacher.

Of course, you know by now that God had a different idea on

the subject. When the altar call was extended, nobody went forward. By the middle of the afternoon, I was miserable. God's Spirit had my heart in His grip and my mind was reeling. I argued with God until bedtime but finally surrendered. I knelt by my grandmother's pull-out sofa sleeper and said "yes" to God's call to preach. I am convinced that I would have never heard God's beckoning call as long as baseball stood between me and Him. To remove this hindrance, God took my baseball talent away drastically and abruptly. So, in the summer of 1978, I parted company with my lifelong love and did not look back. God had given me a new purpose and direction.

Once, about five years later during my seminary education, I faced a test of my commitment to ministry. My neighbor in seminary housing greeted me with intense excitement. He had heard that the Texas Rangers were holding tryouts and wondered if I might be interested. I indicated that it might be fun and asked him to give me the details when he knew the specifics of time and place. I began to daydream of what might happen if I did try out. What if the Rangers saw something they liked? At times, it is difficult to discern when something is God's will or not, but not in this case. God had already closed the door to baseball. So firmly was that door shut, that not only did my neighbor never give me the details, but also I never saw him again. God made sure that our paths never crossed. I saw his car parked in the parking lot and I saw his family from time to time, but I never did see him or speak to him again. God kept me from what may have been a seductive temptation.

The Shadow of Babel

It seemed that God did not intend to allow baseball back into my life, but after seminary, a remarkable thing began to take place. It was as if God said, "Now that I have you fully educated and trained and ready for ministry, I have a gift for you." And He did. He gave baseball back to me. Not as a player (I was far too out-of-shape for that) but as a coach. In most every place I have served, even France, I have coached baseball. One team, with my second son Nathan as the catcher and leadoff batter, won the city championship! It has been a means to share my faith in the Lord Jesus. I have had numerous opportunities to witness and minister to my little leaguers and their families. I have had the privilege of baptizing some of them—quite a few, in fact. I still love baseball, not because of the future it once offered, but because it is a bridge into the lives of people who need to hear the good news of Jesus Christ. Common ground may certainly be transformed into holy ground.

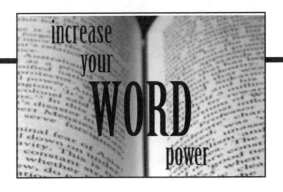

increase your WORD power

1   Most Bible concordances do not list separately all the occasions when the word "all" is used. Most put a note in the preface about the frequency with which it is used being too great to give a complete list, lest the book become unmanageable. This term, however, speaks to the common ground that is the subject of this chapter. "All" is an all-inclusive term. Search your Bible to find some verses that use the term "all."

2   Romans 3:23 says, "For all have sinned and fall short of the glory of God." If you do not already have this verse memorized, do so now. Meditate upon how every person is included in this statement. This immediately gives us common ground with those to whom we speak: We are all sinners.

3   If the preceding point is true, then how must we present the gospel? Should we be condescending to those still trapped in sin? Or, should we identify ourselves with their plight and show them the way of escape through God's grace?

4   What are some ways you can begin to build bridges with your neighbors, friends, and work associates?

CHAPTER NINE

SECRET COMMUNICATION

One day I was flipping through a book that I had read a couple of years before. I was looking for an illustration or a quote that I could use in a sermon. Though I never did find the comment I was searching for, I found something of far greater interest. Inserted between the pages of the book was a piece of paper I had used as a bookmark. On this paper were written the names of five people. I studied the list and recognized it as a list of lost individuals for whom I had been praying. I rejoiced when I realized that four out of the five had been saved and baptized and are now active in the church.

This happens quite often. Not long ago, I pulled an old suit from the back of my closet. I had outgrown it, but my son needed a suit, so he tried it on for size. It was a near-perfect fit, so I checked the pockets before he took it back with him to college. To my surprise, I found a faded piece of yellow paper containing the names of sixteen children and youth. I surveyed the names and again rejoiced with exceeding great joy, for thirteen of those young people had been saved and baptized.

I suppose that this type of thing has happened to me twenty or so times over the years. In similar fashion, before a revival meeting in 1986, the Lakeview Baptist Church in Waco, Texas, compiled a list of lost people in our community for whom we were praying. That list had one hundred names on it. Our average Sunday morning worship attendance was around eighty persons. We discussed a goal for the number of baptisms we would trust God for during our revival services and agreed upon twenty-five. God honored that list and our prayers. We did baptize twenty-five as a direct result of that revival, but we went on to baptize forty-three that year. Most of the forty-three had been on that original list. When we pray for people who do not know the Lord, God works. God honors the faith of a person who is so burdened for the lost that he or she writes the names on a list and prays for them every day. This is not some sort of magic formula, however. You see, when you become burdened for people lost in sin and begin fervently praying for them, God not only works upon their hearts to open them to the gospel, but He works on your heart to go witness to them.

It all begins in the heart of God. He is always working to draw people to Jesus Christ. All over the world, God is actively pursuing lost boys and girls, young people, and adults. He created people for the purpose of fellowship. Even though sin has caused a wide separation between man and himself, God has provided a way of return. Jesus Christ is the way back to God. More than anything, our Father in heaven wants people to be saved. More than anything! The Bible says that He "wants all men to be saved and to come to a knowledge of the truth" (1 Timothy 2:4 NIV). Again, it states that "he is patient with you, not wanting anyone to perish, but everyone to come to repentance" (2 Peter 3:9 NIV). Jesus said, "The Son of Man has come to seek and to save that which was lost" (Luke 19:10). This is the work of the church: to seek the lost so Jesus might save them.

There is, however, a massive shortage of willing witnesses. "The harvest is plentiful, but the workers are few," Jesus reminds us in Matthew 9:37. His answer to this shortage is prayer: "Ask the Lord of the harvest, therefore, to send out workers into his harvest field" (Matthew 9:38 NIV). Someone might ask how it is possible that there are not enough workers, seeing that there is an apparent abundance of preachers and ministers. In response to this question, we must understand that Jesus is not talking about pastors and ministers. He was referring to ordinary Christian men and women who need to be out working in the harvest. The professional ministers will never win our world to Christ Jesus. The task is too big. Furthermore, consider these startling facts. The United States is home to about 5 percent of the world's population but hordes a whopping 95 percent of the world's pastors, ministers, and missionaries. The rest of the world, 95 percent of the population, has access to only 5 percent of those called to the ministry.

One might conclude from these statistics that America is fully evangelized—or at least, everyone has heard the gospel. This would be a false assumption. In fact, America is more lost now than it has ever been. Secular and humanist teachings are prevailing. Cults, religious sects, and new age movements are growing. The reason for this is clear. While there is an abundance of believers in America, the great majority of them are not witnessing. Thousands upon thousands of churches have not seen a baptism in years. There are workers galore, but they are not out in the harvest. They are not witnessing to those lost in sin who live next to them or work in the cubicle across from them.

We must return to our prayer closets and there, in secret prayer, repent of our disobedience to Christ's Great Commission. But here's the rub—that people are not witnessing is evidence that they are not praying! For the most part, Christians have little burden for the lost. This is no surprise, since the only way to get a burden is to get in touch with the heart of God in prayer. If you want a burden for lost people, then make it personal and put it down on paper. Write the names of a few lost friends or family members on a list and pray over those names every day. As you pray, the Holy Spirit will burden your heart over their lost condition. This is just the beginning, however. Praying for the lost is hard and heartbreaking work. Prayer is the difficult but necessary preliminary toil that renders witnessing possible and effective. Witnessing without prayer is like sowing seeds on the sidewalk. The gospel will not penetrate the heart. Praying without witnessing is like a farmer sitting in his easy chair during spring planting and merely thinking about putting seed in the ground. In either case, there will be no harvest. If we truly want to see a turning of the lost to Jesus Christ, then we must speak to God in prayer before we speak to the lost about Jesus.

Praying for the lost is often discouraging. As a lost person draws closer to accepting God's gift of forgiveness through faith in Jesus, the devil grabs on more tightly. Sometimes our lost acquaintances seem to distance themselves from the Lord and us just prior to surrendering to the Lord. I learned this lesson during my first year of college. Several students began meeting together for a time of prayer immediately following dinner each evening. We met in the little "White Chapel" just off the student lounge. Soon, nearly fifty students were attending on a regular basis. We began praying for lost friends by name. Tears often accompanied our prayers as we thought about their need for the Savior. One by one, those we were praying for were being saved. Those after-dinner prayer gatherings became a time of rejoicing as well as a time of burdened weeping. (At the end of this chapter, I will share with you the hard lesson about spiritual leadership that I learned from these White Chapel prayer gatherings.)

One young man became the focus of our prayerful attention. My roommate and I, among many others, fervently prayed for Chris every day. Students and professors alike had witnessed to him. In response, Chris played his heavy metal rock music even louder, cussed more frequently, and pursued more girls. It seemed we were losing ground. As the annual campus revival neared, we rallied our prayer efforts and believed that the evangelistic meetings would not end with Chris still in his lost condition. We prayed and some fasted as the last night of the revival approached. Each evening, we had invited him to attend the revival meetings with us, but he refused our invitations. Our prayers were prevailing, however, and Chris agreed to sit with us for the last meeting. We surrounded him there in the bleachers in the gymnasium and prayed for him throughout the service. During the altar call, many went to the front to pray specifically for Chris, but he did not budge. The service ended; Chris got up and walked off into the night still lost in his sins.

Our little band of prayer warriors regrouped outside the gym and wondered why God had not answered our prayers. We were discouraged and disappointed. We limped back to our dorm, fed those who had been fasting, and decided that Chris was just too hard-hearted.

A few of us returned to the gym and found the evangelist. We told him our problem and asked for some advice. I will never forget what he said, for his response refocused our faith. "Sometimes it is darkest just before the dawn," were his simple words of wisdom. He meant that we should not give up or quit praying and witnessing. His answer encouraged us and we agreed to keep praying for Chris' salvation.

Just before midnight, a frantic knock shook my roommate and me out of our beds. Another student had been sent to tell us that one of Chris' teachers was witnessing to him upstairs in his dorm room. We were asked to go be the prayer support as the teacher witnessed. We ran up the four flights of stairs in great anticipation and found a dimly lit room with a spiritual battle raging inside. The witness talked calmly, quoted Scripture, and invited Chris to surrender his life to Jesus. We prayed, yet Chris resisted. Then, in a split second, Chris fell forward from his chair and was on his knees praying, with heart bowed before the Lord Jesus. He prayed a very honest and sincere prayer inviting Jesus into his life. We rejoiced with him and then flew down those four flights of stairs, hitting only top and bottom steps, to spread the news of Chris' salvation. Prevailing prayer plus persistent witnessing yielded a soul saved for all eternity, but doing so was not easy. Praying is hard work.

American Christians in particular have become accustomed

to an easy brand of faith. We expect all the blessings of God to be hand-delivered to us without much effort on our part. We want people to be saved and complain if people are not walking the aisle, but still we do very little witnessing. We want answers to our prayers but pray very little. We certainly do not want to do anything that might be difficult or that might exact too high a price. In another generation, praying for the lost was often referred to as "travailing in prayer." "Travail" is a word most often used for the process of a woman giving birth. Applied to praying for the lost, it teaches us that souls will not be won to the Lord unless we are actively engaged in the labor of prayer. Praying for the lost is the front lines of the spiritual conflict that rages in this world. All too often we are oblivious to this truth. We are blind soldiers who never enter the fray, leaving loved ones as easy prey for the enemy.

An important aspect of travailing for the lost is fasting. When we fast, we voluntarily give up something, usually food, for a period of time, usually for a day or so, in order to concentrate all our energy and effort on praying. It is an excellent way to keep your prayers centered in Jesus and focused on His provision for the lost. I wonder what would happen in our churches if just a handful of people began sincerely to fast as they travailed for the lost. I truly believe that our churches would be transformed. There would be a renewed excitement for sharing our faith and a fresh empowering from the Holy Spirit for our evangelistic efforts. For far too long, Christians have been silent in witness and have lacked fervor in prayer, neither travailing nor fasting. This silence and prayerlessness condemns us as spiritually lazy and apathetic, but it does not have to remain like this. We can repent of these sins and begin to both pray and witness.

Allow me to suggest three practical steps to help you become a praying, witnessing follower of Jesus. First, establish a prayer list of a few lost friends, family members, or acquaintances. I have never written out such a list and prayed over it without seeing people saved. There is something eternally significant about putting name to paper and committing yourself to prayer. God honors our praying when we get serious enough to ask him every day to save our loved ones. It is best not to make a long list, at first. Begin with three, or maybe five, names. Typically, I keep a list with five names on it. I head the paper with the words, "Focus on Five." I do not remember where I first heard that heading; it is not original with me. If you are a reader, make your list a bookmark that you keep in whatever book you may be currently reading. Pray over your list as you open your book and then again as you replace the bookmark when you are finished. Keep a list with your Bible and use part of your daily Quiet Time to pray for those on your list. Whenever and wherever you can, pray over that list, lifting to God their names and needs.

Second, when you pray, really pray. It does little good to have a list if you are not willing to travail in prayer. Christians often falter when it comes to praying. We talk much about prayer, but spend little time actually praying. I encourage you to pray in these very specific terms: (1) Pray that God will allow you to understand His heart for the lost. Praying in this way will give you a deep burden for those without Jesus. Pray that God will break your heart over your loved ones' lost condition;

(2) Pray that God will prepare and open the hearts of those for whom you pray. Pray that they will be receptive to the gospel and responsive to the conviction of the Holy Spirit. Pray that every hindrance to their being saved will be overcome; and (3) Pray that God will prepare your heart to witness. When we ask God to send someone to a lost friend as a witness, He most often sends us. If you have a fear and/or reluctance to witness, then pray for God to make you willing and bold in witness. Be warned now; if you set yourself to praying for the lost, then you better be prepared to be a witness to those for whom you are praying. Prayer and witness go together.

The third step is to speak. Having prayed, use your voice to invite those on your list to church services. Share your testimony with them. Explain the gospel to them (see Appendix). Invite them to read the Bible with you. Talk to them about spiritual matters. Tell them you are praying for them. If at first they are cold and nonresponsive, do not give up. Keep praying and keep speaking Jesus to them. Listen to their needs and problems. Love them and above all be patient as you persevere in prayer.

When I became the pastor of First Baptist Church, Sesser, Illinois, I noticed rather quickly that a high number of women attended church without their husbands. Of course, some of these were widows, but the vast majority of them were married to men who did not know the Lord. We, therefore, established a list with the names of these lost men—over forty names. We began to pray fervently for those on the list. We made evangelistic visits to their homes and encouraged them to attend church with their wives. Soon, we began to see some fruit from our travailing prayers and our witness. Within two years, we saw nineteen of these men commit their lives to Jesus and become active in the church. There is no magic formula for seeing the lost saved. Putting the name of a lost person on a prayer list is a powerful action, however. It commits the person making the list to faithful prayer and to evangelistic concern. Through our prayers and witness, it brings the power of the Holy Spirit to bear upon the lost person's life. When that happens, people will be saved!

Before turning our attention to the role of the Holy Spirit in our witnessing in the next chapter, allow me to challenge you to add one more element to your prayer life. Most American Christians assume that they are not called to some specific ministry. They believe that if God wants them, He will come knocking on their door but then so live their lives so as not to be home when He calls. To begin with, this is the wrong assumption. Why not assume since God has saved you that He has a special plan for your life. I encourage you to pray a prayer like this: "Lord, where in the world do you want me to serve you?" Most Christians never consider the possibility of being a missionary. If you are a dedicated believer, ask God if He wants you to go to the mission field. This is a very bold prayer—exactly the type of prayer that God loves to hear. When you pray this type of prayer, be sure that you are diligent to listen for His response.

NOTE ON SPIRITUAL LEADERSHIP

I told you earlier in this chapter that I would inform you of the lesson I learned about spiritual leadership from the White Chapel prayer meetings. It was a hard lesson to learn. My roommate, Kevin Chapman, and I were looked upon by the other students involved as the unofficial leaders of the prayer time. We began each meeting by asking for requests and testimonies of answered prayer. Our leadership was not overbearing. We did not dominate the time with our own agenda. The meetings simply needed someone to get the ball rolling and Kevin and I filled that role. After several weeks of prayer and the results mentioned above, Kevin and I talked about our leadership role, wanting to make sure that others did not think that we thought too highly of ourselves. We started asking others to open the meetings with a Scripture reading. Our sincere desire was that the prayer meetings would be an expression of our common faith and not the invention of two individuals. Even when others took the lead in opening the meetings, the students still looked to us for overall leadership. We were too immature to understand that this was an important role we were fulfilling. Prompted by a false sense of humility, we made a decision that I regret to this day. On a beautiful, warm spring day, Kevin and I decided to play tennis after supper instead of going to the White Chapel for prayer. We had calculated that this would force someone else to take the lead and that the group would not be so dependent upon us.

What happened was the exact opposite. Because the group was dependent upon Kevin and me, our absence caused the prayer meetings to come to an abrupt end. No one seemed to think ill of us for playing tennis. There were no hard feelings. Simply put, our absence that one day signaled the end of the prayer meetings. We led by example. The group took our lead and began finding other things to do after dinner.

What I learned was that spiritual leadership is an important matter. It is so important because others are following when you lead. I also learned that God works through leaders. I should have embraced that leadership position and recognized that God had placed Kevin and me there for that very moment in time. While we saw many wonderful blessings through those prayer meetings, I often wonder what would have happened if we had not played tennis that day and the meetings would have continued for a little longer. What lost soul may have yet been won to Christ if we had persevered in prayer? Persistence and faithful endurance go a long way in the realm of prayer and witness. God calls us to persevere in bold witness and in fervent prayer for the lost.

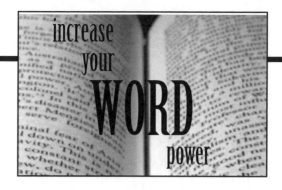

increase your WORD power

1 Read Ephesians 6:10-20. Paul discusses the spiritual warfare we are engaged in as followers of Jesus. Nowhere is this more evident than in our praying for the lost. Notice in verses 18-20 how many references there are to prayer. Circle these references in your Bible.

2 Paul was a very bold and dynamic witness, but never missed an opportunity to enlist others in the task of travailing for the lost. He also asked them to pray for him that he might be even bolder in witness (see Ephesians 6:19). Who can you enlist as a prayer partner?

3 Have you established a prayer list for lost people? Are you faithfully praying over that list? Are you willing to witness to those for whom you are praying?

CHAPTER TEN

OUR NOT-SO-SILENT PARTNER

Does God ever speak in an audible voice? At times He has. Take Moses as an example. When Miriam and Aaron grew tired of playing second and third fiddle, they opposed Moses and criticized him on an insignificant and mute point. Moses' own siblings "began to talk against Moses because of his Cushite wife, for he had married a Cushite" (Numbers 12:1 NIV). They were not truly upset about the issue of Moses' choice of wives, but it was a way to get at Moses and to keep him off-balance for the real battle. Nowhere in Scripture does God take Moses to task over his wife. It just was not an issue, but Miriam and Aaron needed some ammunition and chose something close to his heart. Their real complaint was over leadership in the community of faith. "Has the LORD spoken only through Moses?" they queried. "Hasn't he also spoken through us?" (Numbers 12:2 NIV).

Indeed, He had. Aaron was Moses' mouthpiece. God spoke to Moses, Moses to Aaron, then Aaron to Pharaoh and the children of Israel. Aaron was necessary in part because of Moses' reluctance and initial refusal to be the spokesman himself. Aaron was a go-between. The Bible calls Miriam a prophetess. She encouraged the Israelites through song and dance (see Exodus 15). Yes, indeed, God had spoken through both Miriam and Aaron, but they had missed the point. God's relationship with Moses was different than his relationship with either of them. God explained himself to them: "When a prophet of the LORD is among you, I reveal myself to him in visions; I speak to him in dreams. But this is not true of my servant Moses; he is faithful in all my house. With him I speak face to face, clearly and not in riddles; he sees the form of the LORD" (Numbers 12:6-8 NIV). God put an exclamation point on this statement by causing Miriam to become leprous. She got the point, and she and Aaron never wavered on this issue again. Moses was *the* leader because God spoke to him face to face—audible voice included.

When you and I try to hear from God on some specific issue in our lives, it nearly always seems that God is speaking to us in riddles. There is a clue here and there, but we are often left to guess as to what we should do. Of course, it is at this point that faith becomes the issue. Are we willing to trust God's leadership even with little apparent light on the subject? There have been many times, however, when I wish He had given more light, better clues, and spoken in an audible voice. If He had, all doubt would have been erased, but so might have my faith. If God spoke audibly on every little issue, where would the faith be? Besides, I would most likely begin to act like the children of Israel who wearied under God's spoken revelation and quickly turned away from following His spoken word to them (see Exodus 20:18-23 and Exodus 32). I have learned to trust God for the light He gives along the path of my life, knowing that He always gives enough light and information to take the next step.

I cannot say that I have ever heard the audible voice of God. Once, like the crowd in John 12, I thought I heard something like thunder in the distance, but then, it really was just thunder. On two occasions, however, I have heard God speak distinctly, something like a voice in my head and heart, not audible, but unambiguous nonetheless. So precise was His unspoken voice that I knew it was His. Let me differentiate between hearing God's voice through preaching, reading the Scriptures, and general impressions given while praying, and hearing a clear, indisputable, yet inaudible word from God. God has spoken to me countless times through sermons, books, and prayers. If I am spiritually alert, He speaks to me every day as I read His Word. But twice, I have had the undeniable impression that God has spoken to me directly and with precise words.

The first occurrence was toward the end of my seminary education. I was pastoring a small church outside of Waco, Texas. I drove 160 miles round-trip four days a week as I completed my Master's level theology degree. I had a young family and a growing church. I was busy and fatigued. We made visits in area homes one evening per week, inviting families to our church services. On one evening our outreach attendance was sparse and I ended up going out by myself. I attempted two or three visits and found no one home, but that suited me fine. I wanted nothing more than to return home and relax. Just blocks away from home, I stopped at an intersection and let a car pass. A right turn took me home to my easy chair. God said, "Turn left. Go see Christy." I heard it in my spirit as clearly as I have heard anything in my life. It was God's Spirit speaking to my spirit. Jesus called him "the Spirit of Truth," then added, "you know him, for he lives with you and will be in you" (John 14:17 NIV).

Contrary to many today who claim to hear God's voice especially clear, the message I received was not some new revelation or truth to be shared with the masses in order to convince them to send me money. God's Spirit was directing my steps to a lost and grieving young woman. God's heart was broken over her need and His Spirit sent me to her to minister and witness. Several weeks prior, Christy's husband of just six months had been tragically killed in a traffic accident. She had lost the love of her life and her world was spinning out of control. Not only had God's Spirit directed me to go see her (at her mother-in-law's home), but He had prepared her heart as well. She was receptive to the gospel message and gave her life to Jesus that night! I am glad that I did not race home to my easy chair.

Several months after this encounter, I heard God's voice even more distinctly. Again, it was not an audible voice, but one spoken to my mind and heart through His Spirit. My wife and I had been dealing with the International Mission Board about missionary service. At first, we thought that God was calling us to serve in Africa, but we quickly sensed His leading in another direction. While attending Missions Week at Glorieta Baptist Conference Center in New Mexico, we met three missionary couples serving in Paraguay. We listened with great interest to their stories and studied their pictures and artifacts from their adopted country. Through them the Holy Spirit began tugging at our hearts. We could not avoid the persistent thought that God was calling us to service in that South American country. We returned home with great anticipation of being appointed as missionaries to Paraguay. One afternoon, not long after our return home, we received a phone call from Jim, our Candidate Consultant from the International Mission Board, who informed us that the door to Paraguay was closed to us. Another couple would be filling that need. We were disappointed and confused. It seemed God was speaking in riddles again. Had we not been seeking God in prayer? Had we not felt His leading toward Paraguay?

After reassuring us in our pursuit of missionary service, Jim told us that he needed to send us some new personnel requests to look over. These requests came from the various mission fields and indicated what personnel needs they had. I told him to send us some from other South American countries (at least we knew the general area to which God was calling us). He told me that he would get them in the mail that day and then added, "I'm going to send you a request from France. Just look it over. If you're not interested, that's alright."

I remember telling my wife how odd it was that he just threw France into the mix at the last moment (just another clue along the way), but we did not give it another thought as we anxiously waited for the personnel requests to arrive. When they did, each one was marked "urgent need." We spent that day reading and re-reading the descriptions of each country's culture, the missionary force currently serving, the type of work to be done, etc. We arranged and rearranged the stack according to our latest insight and impression. It was a back-and-forth, pull-and-push contest of global proportions, but always France was on the bottom of the stack—dead last. A couple more days of prayer and sorting and rearranging left us with what appeared to be an ever more settled picture—that is, until late one afternoon as we were preparing to go out for the evening. I had gone to my office at our church next door while I waited for Judy to get ready. When I returned to the house and headed for my chair, I heard God speak as I sat down. At first, I thought it had been audible, so clear was the message. God did not say much. He did not need to. He simply asked, "Have you considered France?"

From that moment, we really considered France! God had spoken by His indwelling Spirit, calling us to our field of missionary service. As we became convinced that God was leading us to France, we began to have a little fun with the decision-making process. I said before that, prior to this communication from God as we stacked and re-stacked the personnel requests, France was always on the bottom. Now, we could not escape it. We closed our eyes and shuffled the requests like a deck of cards. When we opened our eyes, France was on top. We threw the papers into the air; France landed on top. We threw them up again, all the others were face down, but France was face-up. No matter what we tried, France came out on top. Of course, by this time in the process and after much prayer, we were already convinced of God's will for us to go to France. We would have never resorted to such game-like actions if we were not already sure where God was leading us. Over and over, however, God reassured us. He had spoken and that is always enough!

The Shadow of Babel

Twice and only twice has God ever spoken directly to me with an almost audible voice. On both occasions, God's concern was centered upon those lost without Christ Jesus. Let me add, that of the thousands of dreams I have had over my lifetime, only one is of any significance. Most of my dreams are nothing more than a ridiculous mixture of the events of the day or some anxiety mingled with greasy food. The theme of that one significant dream was, as you might have guessed, God's concern for a world without Jesus. In it I saw man standing on the threshold of eternity. On one side was all the glory of heaven, beautiful beyond description; on the other a torrent of what seemed to be molten lava, flowing toward the pit of hell itself. The man in my dream was condemned to hell, but he protested, claiming that he had not been given a chance to decide. A voice said, "Choose now." The man looked toward all the beauty of heaven and then he looked toward that river of souls departing to the horrors of hell. Back and forth he looked as he stood on the threshold of a great door. I realized as I dreamed that he could not make up his mind. So stark was the contrast between the two eternal states and yet he was undecided. I sat straight up in my bed, startled by the dream. Now awake, I concluded that the dream was a type of parable about the plight of man. Left to himself, he is unable to decide to follow even a clearly marked path to God's blessings. Faced with the horrors of hell, people will choose hell, or at best are reluctant to choose heaven. Of course, God does not give people a second chance after they die. That is where you and I come in. Before death claims the souls of those around us, we must urgently encourage them to trust Jesus as their Savior and commit by faith to follow Him as Lord. This is where the Holy Spirit is so vitally involved.

The Holy Spirit yearns to bring people to Jesus Christ through us. He is the ultimate witness, for that is His role. Consider the words of Jesus concerning His Spirit: "When the Counselor comes, whom I will send to you from the Father, the Spirit of Truth who goes out from the Father, he will *testify* about me. And you also must *testify*" (John 15:26-27 NIV, italics mine). The Spirit continually testifies about Jesus. It is the presence of the Holy Spirit in our lives that compels and empowers us to witness. We are partners in evangelism with the Holy Spirit. He speaks through our words of witness.

Let's review for a moment the role of the Holy Spirit in communicating the gospel of Jesus Christ. Just prior to His ascension, Jesus told His followers that it was now their responsibility to proclaim His death and resurrection to all the nations, for "you are witnesses of these things. I am going to send you what my Father has promised; but stay in the city until you have been clothed with power from on high" (Luke 24:48-49 NIV). Continuing his account of the life and ministry of Jesus, Luke quotes his Lord again, "You will receive power when the Holy Spirit has come upon you; and you shall be My witnesses . . . to the remotest part of the earth" (Acts 1:8).

Of course, the Holy Spirit came powerfully upon those first disciples on the Day of Pentecost, enabling them to speak of Jesus that day. Peter explained the phenomenon by quoting the prophet Joel who said, "In the last days, God says, I will pour out my Spirit on all people" (Acts 2:17 NIV). At the conclusion of

Peter's sermon, three thousand souls were saved. The church in Jerusalem continued to grow and the gospel spread in spite of fierce opposition. New voices, like those of Stephen and Philip, were added to the crescendo of gospel proclamation. Then, in Antioch, where a strong nucleus of believers worshiped, the Holy Spirit said, "Set apart for Me Barnabas and Saul for the work to which I have called them" (Acts 13:2). The Holy Spirit had been, since the Day of Pentecost, raising up witnesses and sending them out. God's Spirit is still in the business of raising up witnesses.

Having called forth an army of witnesses, the Spirit directed them as a general his troops, moving this one here and another one there. It was the Spirit who told Philip to go into the desert and find the chariot of the Ethiopian eunuch. It was the Spirit who forbid Paul's band of missionaries to go one direction and then another before He opened a door of ministry and witness in Philippi (see Acts 16). The Holy Spirit not only calls forth witnesses, but He sends them out to specific locations and to particular people.

Even so, the Holy Spirit's work in witnessing is not complete. Once He has directed the steps of His witnesses and gets them into a position to speak for Jesus, He then gives them the words to say. The Spirit inspires our witnessing conversations. Through our minds, hearts, and mouths, the Holy Spirit calls the lost to Christ. Jesus said, "When he comes, he will convict the world of guilt in regard to sin and righteousness and judgment" (John 16:8 NIV). In other words, through the vehicle of our speech and the inner witness to the spirit of man, the Holy Spirit convicts the lost of the sin that separates them from God, convinces them that righteousness is found only in Jesus Christ, and condemns them if they eventually refuse to trust Him for salvation. The Holy Spirit is the ultimate witness, but He will not do it without our voices and words. God has chosen to include those of us who follow Jesus in His plan to redeem the world. Each new believer joins the ranks of witnesses and lends his or her voice as an instrument in the Spirit's hands.

A silent partner is usually someone behind the scenes who lends support but keeps out of the way. The Holy Spirit, however, has taken a prominent role in witnessing. He is not really a silent partner, even though we may never hear His audible voice. Ironically, Christians have been the silent ones in the partnership. While the Spirit yearns for the lost to be saved, believers have quieted their voices. Countless Christians have decided not to speak on Jesus' behalf. The prophet Jeremiah tried to still the voice of God spoken through him and found that he could not. He said, "If I say, 'I will not mention him or speak any more in his name,' his word is in my heart like a fire, a fire shut up in my bones. I am weary of holding it in; indeed, I cannot" (Jeremiah 20:9 NIV). My prayer for you is that the Holy Spirit's voice of witness through you will be as a fire in your bones!

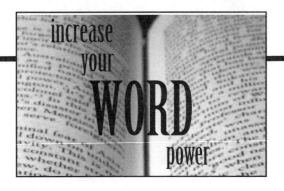

increase your WORD power

1 John 16:8-11 speaks of the role of the Holy Spirit in bringing lost people to salvation, convicting them of their sin, convincing them that righteousness comes only through faith in Jesus, and condemning them if they refuse to believe. Think back to the time of your conversion. How was the Holy Spirit convicting you of your sin? What did He do to convince you that you needed Jesus?

2 Romans 6:23 says, "For the wages of sin is death, but the free gift of God is eternal life in Christ Jesus our Lord." The consequence of unbelief is eternal separation from God. God offers salvation from sin and death through Jesus. Is it any wonder then that the Holy Spirit is so very active to draw people to Jesus? Are you allowing the Spirit to move through you toward the lost around you?

3 Practice listening for God's still, small voice. Pray and listen. Be sensitive to the promptings and nudges of the Holy Spirit. If you have an impression that you need to speak to someone about Jesus, you can be sure that this is the work of the Holy Spirit. With the assurance that He is prompting you, open your mouth in bold witness.

CHAPTER ELEVEN

CROSSING THE CULTURAL DIVIDE

During the 1980s, *The Cosby Show* was a cultural phenomenon. Life virtually shut down at 7:00 P.M. CST on Thursday evenings. Everybody, it seems, was tuned in to see the latest installment of Bill Cosby's hit TV sitcom. Everybody but me, that is. Now, don't get me wrong, I loved the show, but I seldom was able to watch more than just a few minutes here and there. You see, our church had its outreach visitation on Thursday evenings. We would meet at the church at 7:00 P.M., pray briefly, and then go out in teams with our visitation assignments. I would usually arrive at the first house ten or fifteen minutes into the show.

We were highly ineffective in our outreach. We were invading a sacred time. Most of the time when I made visits in the community, the residents would receive me warmly and, if their television sets were on, they would politely turn them off so we could visit. Nobody turned Cosby off, however. They would not turn the volume down. They would not turn their eyes away from the TV. It was obvious that we had come at a bad time and they resented the intrusion. We were trying to say the right words—words of witness and encouragement—but we were saying them at the wrong time. Week by week we met with the same response and hostility was growing in the community. Rather than bringing a blessing, we had become a nuisance.

We had a very difficult decision to make. Should we persist in making our visits on Thursdays and count it a privilege to be scorned for the sake of the gospel or, heaven forbid, should we change our visitation program to another night of the week. "But we have always had visitation on Thursday evenings. We can't make visits on another night. That's heresy!" Such was the emotional response of our church members. I took a deep breath and decided to move our outreach program to Tuesday nights. There were two wonderful results of this decision. First, I was finally able to watch an entire episode of *The Cosby Show* (some even accused me of changing visitation nights just so I could watch the show). Second, people actually started getting saved.

On Tuesdays the television sets were turned off and attention was given to what we were saying. God was at work! We had been saying the right things but at the wrong time. When we said the right words at the right time, people heard and understood and responded by faith in the Lord Jesus Christ. It can be argued that there is never a wrong time to share the good news of Jesus. Indeed, we ought to be ready to share the gospel message in season and out of season—that is, at all times. The point I am trying to make here is that we should take care to speak when people are listening. The result of our decision to change our outreach night was that more people were baptized that year into the fellowship of the church than had ever been in any previous year. When we became sensitive to the culture into which we were proclaiming the gospel, doors opened and lives were transformed.

For missionaries who serve in other lands, culture presents a host of problems. Culture may be defined as "a way of thinking, feeling, believing. It is the group's knowledge stored up for future use."[17] Louis J. Luzbetak, in his book *The Church and Cultures*, defines culture as "a design for living. It is a plan according to which society adapts itself to its physical, social, and ideational environment."[18] My wife and I experienced "culture shock" the first few months that we were in France. Part of the problem was that of expectations, perceptions, and preferences. France presents itself as a western nation like our own, and one finds many similarities between the two. Those similarities are mostly superficial, however. The nuances of different cultural perspectives can send a person into a state of shock. Expecting those similarities to work themselves out in exactly the same way as in the missionaries' home culture, they soon discover that the apparent similarities are really nothing alike.

Not long after arriving in France, we purchased a television set. Our language coach told us to turn it on and leave it on, for it would help tune our ears to the French language. Truly it did. One afternoon, a rerun of *Happy Days*, dubbed into French, came on. That show was a personal favorite of mine when I was younger. We sat down with our children, ages five and three, to watch. At a commercial break, we could not believe our eyes. There on the screen was a naked women selling orange juice of all things. Judy reached to cover my eyes as I reached to cover my children's. We were shocked! The similarities proved to be worlds apart. Our expectations and preconceived notions did not anticipate a major deviation from what we were used to seeing on TV. Our perception of French television changed drastically in that moment. We concluded that we preferred the American television experience over the French version, which was similar yet drastically different. Cultures had collided.

We must go through this same process of understanding cultural differences in every witnessing conversation, even here in the United States. There are perhaps greater obstacles here. Overseas, you expect differences and when you find them, the initial shock wears off as you adjust your perceptions. At home, we do not anticipate these cultural differences, but they exist nonetheless. I am not talking primarily about regional differences; we expect those minor distinctions. The problem arises when we do not realize that there exists a cultural divide between Christians and the average non-Christian, unchurched individual. We think differently, behave differently, move in different circles, and perceive things in dissimilar ways. The person to whom we are witnessing may look like us, dress like us, and talk like us but may think in a totally different way. A lost person's worldview is at odds with a Christian's worldview.

David Hesselgrave identifies worldview as "the way people see reality . . . the way people see or perceive the world, the way they 'know' it to be."[19] Paul Hiebert explains further, "The basic assumptions about reality which lie behind the beliefs and behavior of a culture are sometimes called a worldview."[20] Hesselgrave quotes Hiebert as he personalizes the definition: "Our worldview, then, is 'the way we see ourselves in relation to all else. Conversely, it is the way we see all else in relation to ourselves!'"[21] Followers of Jesus and lost people often have diamet-

rically opposed perceptions of reality. To be effective in our witness we must recognize this basic difference and attempt to cross the cultural divide that separates their way of thinking from ours.

Unless we understand what we may call subcultural variants of the larger culture, we may not communicate the gospel well. These subcultural groups are smaller groupings which are "the primary units that [define] norms and behavior . . . the sources of information that [provide] paradigms for understanding the social, spiritual, and natural world."[22] As we share our faith, we may experience these subcultural differences as an obstacle to our witness. We may share the same culture with those who are like us in race and nationality, but our subcultural worldviews may be vastly different. As a result of these differences, we may be shocked by the response to our message—that is, the response may not match our expectations. This shock may cause us to recoil from a relationship with a person who desperately needs the Lord.

I recently ministered to a family whose daughter had been seriously injured in a freak accident at school. There was a real danger of blindness in one eye as a result. She was a very talented athlete and the entire community rallied around the family. The girl's family never attended church and had some extremely rough edges. Every church in town reached out to the girl and her family in prayer and encouragement. Her family was keenly aware of the prayers being offered. After surgery to repair part of the damage, the prognosis was good for the recovery of sight but bleak as to the likelihood of resuming any athletic activity. People kept praying, however, and four weeks later she was back

in uniform. It was a wonderful work of God upon her life. A Christian man in town, while talking to the girl's father, commented that his daughter's recovery was an answer to prayer. The father's natural—his subcultural—response was a very blatant "No s$#&!! (Excuse my French). This response came after the family had begun attending our church. This man recognized that God had worked and was thankful, yet his subculture of hard living and vulgar speech was at odds with our Christian lifestyle and word choice.

Church members usually want people like this to clean up their act before they come into the church. This is why many people, like this man and his family, do not often visit our churches. They know how we feel about them. Only when we accept their subculture at face value (not to condone it or justify it) and witness across this cultural divide, will people like this come to Christ. We cannot expect non-Christian people to act like Christians before they are. If we are to witness successfully to them, we must accept them as they are. Is not *Just As I Am* one of our favorite hymns of invitation? God accepts us just as we are as we approach Him for saving grace, but thankfully, He does not leave us like we are. When we accept people in spite of their cultural and worldview differences, they may listen more attentively to our witness and be saved. Once they are saved, God will begin to transform their character and mold a Christian worldview into their hearts and minds.

Even if we do not distance ourselves from people who are not like us, we may yet fail to convey the gospel in a culturally significant way. We may say the right words, but the words are

as we understand them. We wrongly assume our hearers understand them in the same way. A vivid reminder of this has become apparent even in my own writing. Throughout this book I have referred to "lost people" and to evangelizing a "lost world." By "lost" I am referring to those who do not have a personal relationship with God through faith in Jesus Christ. They have not repented of their sins or surrendered control of their lives to the Lord Jesus. You probably have had the same definition of terms in your mind as you read. If I used the words "lost world" to my youngest son a few years ago, his mind might have conjured up an image of an island in the Pacific Ocean overrun with dinosaurs, á la *Jurassic Park.*

If those we are witnessing to do not grasp the Christian nuance of our terminology, the message gets lost in the words. This raises an important issue that David Hesselgrave refers to as *contextualization,* or "the process of adapting the Christian message to people of other cultures."[23] We must put the good news into the context of the lost people we want to reach, giving them "the capacity to respond meaningfully to the gospel within the framework"[24] of their unique situation. Understand, then, that when we contextualize the gospel we are not changing the message but the manner in which we share it. For instance, much has been discovered recently about how non-literate people groups learn. Storytelling plays a vital role in this process. If we were to attempt to reach such oral learners by employing the techniques of Greek rhetoric or logic, we would not be effective at all in communicating the great truths of the gospel to them. Our message may well be lost upon their ears, never penetrating their hearts and minds. Tell them the stories of the Bible, however, and the Holy Spirit begins to open them to God's rich love for them. Hesselgrave says,

> Contextualization can be thought of as the attempt to communicate the message of the person, works, word, and will of God in a way that is faithful to God's revelation, especially as it is put forth in the teachings of Holy Scripture, and that is meaningful to respondents in their respective cultural contexts.[25]

Because this task of putting the gospel into the context of those we want to reach is so daunting, it is important that the missionary on cross-cultural mission fields and the witness on his own home soil understand culture—both his own culture and that of those he hopes to reach. To be effective witnesses we must engage ourselves in a study of these cultures in order to develop "cultural self-awareness."[26] Only as we understand our own culture can we begin to comprehend another, and only in the comprehension of that other culture may we begin to communicate Jesus in a way people from that other culture can understand.

This is not only true on distant mission fields, however. This work of contextualization must take place even if you are merely crossing the street to share the gospel with someone who is basically just like you.

Recognizing that lost people are different (even culturally

different) from Christians has been a long process. Books like Lee Strobel's *Inside the Mind of Unchurched Harry and Mary* and *Surprising Insights from the Unchurched* and *The Unchurched Next Door* by Thom Rainer are helping God's people understand how to think like people without Christ and how to communicate Jesus in a way they can understand. Once these cultural differences are understood, barriers begin to collapse and we realize that culture can even be an ally that helps us better explain and interpret Jesus. Many dedicated Christians are attempting to understand the postmodern mind-set in order to better communicate the gospel to those who think this way. Postmoderns have a vastly different worldview than did the preceding generations. Witnessing must be approached on a different level, or we will not win a hearing with them. Understanding how they think gives the Christian witness a foothold as he tries to communicate the truths of Christ Jesus.

To give a practical application to this concept, let me urge you not to distance yourself from non-Christian friends and acquaintances. If you have been a believer for only a short time, the friends you have been spending time with need to hear the good news that you have come to accept for yourself. You may be the only Christian friend they have. Studies have shown that the longer you are a Christian, the fewer non-Christian friends you have. If you have been a Christian for some time now, then take steps to cultivate friendships with those who are unchurched. Get to know them and accept them as they are and love them unconditionally. You can have deeply meaningful relationships with those who are lost in sin without compromising your morals or your beliefs. Build bridges into their culture and worldview and communicate Jesus in ways they can understand. Meet them where they are and lead them across the cultural divide to Jesus.

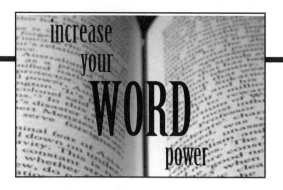

increase your WORD power

1 Read Philippians 2:5-11, paying special attention to verses 6-7. Jesus, though "He existed in the form of God, . . . emptied Himself, taking the form of a bond-servant." Jesus crossed the cultural divide in order to identify with us and save us from our sin.

2 Think about the last witnessing conversation you had. Were there any terms that you might need to clarify? We must strive to use words that lost people can understand. Justification, sanctification, and similar theological terms are informative in Christian discipleship classes but are too complicated for witnessing encounters.

3 Do you know a person who thinks completely differently than you do? What steps could you take to begin to understand his/her worldview? Pray that the Holy Spirit will enable you to reach across these differences with a clear and consistent witness.

CHAPTER TWELVE

MARKETPLACE NOISES

I would have failed the devil's first temptation of Jesus in the wilderness. I love bread. I would have jumped at the opportunity to turn stones into loaves of steaming hot, delicious bread. I can smell those desert-baked loaves now, but I must remind myself that Jesus declared as He resisted the devil, "Man does not live on bread alone, but on every word that comes from the mouth of God" (Matthew 4:4 NIV).

Bread became for me a useful tool while in language school. France is full of patisseries and one is located within sniffing distance of every house. Afternoon bakery smells beckoned me to leave my formal language study of sentence structure and rules of grammar in order to hunt for bread. It became a daily routine. Late each afternoon, lines would form outside these neighborhood bakeries as people prepared for dinner. I joined them in line, waiting my turn to place my order—*Un pain, s'il vous plait*—which meant, "Give me one of those long loaves of bread, please." I would rarely fight the temptation of nibbling off the end on the way home.

Although I loved the *pain* and its smaller but equally delicious *baguette*, my appetite for bread pushed me to purchase other items as well. This is where my language learning flourished. Not knowing the names of all the different types of bread, I would have to ask, listen very carefully, try to repeat what I had heard, and then pay for my selection. This was often much harder than it might appear. I was still an infant in the French language and struggled to comprehend the mixture of vowels and consonants as the busy cashier blended and contracted the syllables that comprised the words I was attempting to hear and use. To make matters worse, the noise that filtered in off the busy street and the voices of the other bread-lovers distorted the message further. At first, I resorted to paying with large bills so that I knew that I had given the cashier enough. The result was buckets full of change. It was a great day when I first understood the price to be paid and was able to present the exact change. I should have received a standing ovation, for I was learning the language in spite of all the marketplace noises.

The Great Commission pushes us out our front doors and comfort zones into a busy and noisy world. Jesus said, "As you go, make disciples." He assumed that witnessing would take place in the normal circuits of our busy schedules. Just as my best language learning was not done in a classroom but out on the sidewalks and in the shops where people were speaking French, so our most effective witnessing will be out in the midst of people as they work and shop and play. I would have preferred a noiseless bread store in which to learn, but I learned best as I fought through the surrounding clamor of voices and sounds.

Witnessing is probably best done in quiet spots with no distractions, but those places are hard to find. We must learn to witness where people are and when we can access them. We cannot always find them at home on the given weeknight of our church outreach program. Not long ago, our church outreach director was given the name of a young couple who did not attend church. On four consecutive Tuesday nights a group of visitors went by their home to invite them to church and to begin a witnessing conversation, only to find them away for the evening. Tuesday night was the only time we tried to reach them. That just happened to be the night they bowled. After four attempts we quit trying. I wonder, though, how many Christians crossed their paths in a given day. If we would alter our perceptions of when to witness, we might find limitless opportunities to share the gospel.

Indeed, opportunities abound if we are willing to seize them. This requires adopting a lifestyle of witnessing as opposed to a programmed approach. When we program our witnessing, we fit it into our schedules when it best suits us, usually one night a week. On the positive side, such programs mobilize a part of the church for outreach. The negatives outweigh the positives, however, limiting evangelism to a very small sliver of time and an even smaller segment of the church. Evangelism programs attract only a few faithful members and guilt is usually their motivation for participating.

Recently, I re-read a classic book on evangelism. My seminary professor, Roy J. Fish, a great personal soul-winner and a wonderful teacher of evangelism, updated J. E. Conant's book, *Every Member Evangelism*, written in 1922. In the preface to his updated version, *Every Member Evangelism for Today*, Fish writes, "every church member ought to be equipped for, and to engage in, personal evangelism."[27] I could not agree more; in fact, it is the most basic idea behind the book you are now reading. Over the years many attempts have been made by pastors and church leaders to mobilize the entire church membership to witness. Conant and Fish relate this process of enlistment and its end result:

> Today many earnest and consecrated pastors are heartbroken over the failure of their congregations to reach people for Christ in any significant numbers. More than one such pastor has gone from his knees to his pulpit, surcharged with passion for lost humanity and with a divinely given yearning for his people to be possessed by the same passion. He has set before them the call to share the Good News of Jesus until it has seemed as though no one could fail to respond. Often this same pastor has risen to such an intensity of appeal that it seemed as though the Son of God himself was pouring out his own yearning for a lost world through human heart and lips.

> As the pastor has pleaded with his people, he has seen the evidence in their faces of a determination to give their lives as never before to the work of witnessing. Indeed, he has seen many of them make a solemn public pledge before God that

seeking to win the lost to Christ would be the main purpose of their lives from that day forward. Then as he watched them leave the service and scatter into the field, he has anticipated such results from that hour as the church has never before seen.

But he is doomed to sad and bitter disappointment. The enthusiastic resolutions of that holy hour seemed to vanish before the next Sunday. Perhaps the pastor could detect a little increased activity on the part of a small handful of his most faithful people, but he was compelled to acknowledge that little, if anything, of increased results in soul-winning ever came from the service which had seemed to promise so much.[28]

My heart breaks over the truth of these paragraphs. I have been one of those pastors pleading for soul-winners and seeing little outcome from my effort. I was surprised, however, at the authors' conclusion as to why so little effect was wrought, stating that "it was not lack of a purpose so much as 'lack of a program' that accomplished their defeat."[29] Perhaps in the 1920s and 1970s when the book was first written, then updated, more programmed evangelism[30] was needed. Subsequent decades have, to my perception, yielded very little evidence that programs are the answer. The authors cite the Great Commission to reinforce their call for a better program of evangelism. Churches have proven, for the most part, that programs, even better programs, yield some but relatively little results. To my understanding, Christ's Great Commission was not the instituting of a church program but a call for every believer to be a lifestyle witness—that is, witnessing must be incorporated into the very fabric of their lives. There is a vast difference between what some call "lifestyle evangelism" which basically emphasizes a nonverbal witness of meeting needs through acts of caring (showing people the love of Jesus) and witnessing as a lifestyle which is heavy on our verbal witness (telling people about Jesus). "As you go" is a rendering of the Greek participle of the verb "to go" and encapsulates the biblical concept of a lifestyle of witnessing. This participle still carries the weight of an imperative and may not be interpreted as optional. An "as you go" mentality encourages believers to evangelize as they go about their daily routines. It also commands them to go out into a marketplace full of lost people.

The marketplace is exactly where the apostle Paul wanted to be. When he was waiting in Athens for the arrival of his missionary colleagues, he witnessed "in the marketplace day by day with those who happened to be there" (Acts 17:17 NIV). In Jesus' parable of the great banquet (Luke 14:15-24), He urged his followers to "go out at once into the streets and lanes of the city." Being out there in the hustling, bustling city, or on the square of the county seat, or even on the farm-to-market roads of rural towns and villages can leave us feeling uncomfortable and intimidated. It is easy to let our voice of witness be drowned out by all the noises of a busy world. We might even begin to think that our voices are insignificant or irrelevant.

Perhaps Paul just wanted to do some sightseeing in Athens, but as he walked through that ancient jewel of the Greek world, he could not help but notice the lostness of the people. The Bible says that "his spirit was being provoked within him" (Acts 17:16). Luke connects verses sixteen and seventeen with a conjunction that indicates that the reason he began dialoguing with the people in the marketplace (v. 17) was because his spirit was being stirred (v. 16). As he was proclaiming Jesus and the resurrection, he was invited to the Areopagus where every novel philosophical idea was debated. There, in that austere setting, Paul called the men of Athens to repentance and faith in Jesus. The result was that most thought him to be out of his mind, but some believed and began to follow the Lord Jesus. When we go out into the marketplaces of our cities and towns, we can expect the same kind of response. Many may think we are crazy and sneer their ridicule at us, but some will believe and follow Jesus. Paul decided that his message was the most relevant message of his day and, consequently, entered boldly into the marketplace of Athens and proclaimed his faith in the most prominent gathering place in the city. We carry a simple message to the lost masses, but its simplicity does not mean it is irrelevant. Our message is the most significant word anyone could possibly hear.

How can we compete with a world that is infatuated with high-tech gadgets and the information explosion? In my own lifetime, I have seen music conveyance move from long playing albums to eight-tracks to cassette tapes to compact disks to i-pods and mp3 players. I used to buy albums of twelve to sixteen songs that took up a space of a square foot on my desk. My wife has an i-pod nano that is a square inch in size and holds about 250 songs. Most people have something—cell phones or headphones—seemingly attached to their ears at all times. How are we to gain a hearing? It is hard to get a word in edgewise. If only we could *Bluetooth* our gospel message straight to their brains. As it is, the gospel is just one among millions of pieces of information that bombard our audience each day. We must, therefore, take our voices boldly into that domain. We must make ourselves heard above the din. While the lost and unchurched have relegated the gospel to a secondary or even a tertiary status (I will give it some attention when my life calms down a bit.), we must proclaim it as *the* only essential truth. We must shout Christ to an indifferent world that has always tried to drown out our message of hope.

Very early, every other Saturday morning, I would pack up boxes of books, pamphlets, and tracts and transport them to the public *Marché* (somewhat like a flea market) in Morsang-sur-Orge in the southern suburbs of Paris. There, under a multicolored canopy, several church members and I would arrange our materials on a foldout table. Often fighting rain and cold temperatures, we established a gospel presence in the midst of the disinterest of a godless culture. Basically, we were ignored. Sometimes a person might glance down at our display but then quickly look away. Others who noticed us would frown and still others would offer scoffing laughter. We were a lone and lonely voice in that marketplace. Few, if any, would stop and talk for a moment, usually sharing some hurt or heartache, desperate for help and attention. Those were priceless moments when a connection was made and the gospel became real to a person in need. Most passed by never realizing how much they truly needed the One we proclaimed. When business was slow, I would leave our table of literature in the hands of my helpers and wander through the maze of booths and stands. It was a tremendous sight: flowers in springtime, summer, and autumn; vegetables and fruit of all varieties and sizes; fresh fish that lent their unique aroma to all who passed by; meat being chopped and cut and wrapped in white butcher paper; household goods and craft items all mixed together in a cultural extravaganza. I learned to pay attention to the people. Oblivious to eternal questions, they went about their business in matter-of-fact simplicity. Making selections that would garnish their Sunday tables, they always had time to stop and chat with friends or argue some political issue. When I talked with them, however, they always needed to hurry on to their next purchase.

Occasionally, we would do something special just to make them look our way. Our youth group, with the help of two short-term missionaries from England, performed a skit and sang some praise choruses. A person who watched and listened that day came to our worship service the next. We counted it a great success! On other days, armed with flyers announcing a special concert or event, we would pass among the people and offer our printed information. Not long after, you could see the *Marché* littered with our crumpled, ignored invitations. The marketplace is a tough place to be, but we must infiltrate the world of the lost with the good news of Jesus Christ. Even if they do not want to listen, we must continue to shout forth the message.

Our marketplace witness must be much more than a booth set up once a week. What I am advocating is a lifestyle of witnessing wherever you are and whenever you can. As you go through your daily routine, you have many opportunities to speak up for Jesus. Think of the stops you make on the way to and from work. You may pull into your neighborhood food and gas mart to fill your tank or buy a cup of steaming hot coffee. Most likely, you are in the habit of sharing pleasantries with those who serve you in these instances. Over time, if you will apply yourself, you get to know these people. We must move past the pleasant, innocuous comments about weather, traffic, and sports and point them to the Savior. In that setting, I do not recommend an in-depth explanation of gospel truth (unless God providentially gives you a divine appointment). Your schedule and theirs would not permit that, but a few words from day to day that speak of Jesus and underline your faith may open the door someday for a deeper conversation. Have you ever just asked someone like this if they had anything you could pray for? Try it. Most people are shocked but polite and appreciate that you care enough to ask. Some will share a quick need. Promise them that you will pray for them and then follow up later by asking how things turned out. You will be surprised how this simple act might open doors for a more intense spiritual conversation. These brief, pinpoint witnessing opportunities add up over time, helping the person become more aware of who Jesus is and how He can meet their needs.

My point is this: we know people who are not our close friends or neighbors or work associates but with whom we have ᴧmost daily contact. We may not know where they live, so a week-night visit through the church's outreach program will not reach them. You have the opportunity for a short time each day or so to find your voice for Jesus. Would you agree with me that it is easier not even to try in those situations? We are in a hurry; they are at work. There may be other customers in line. Why should we bother? The simple but profound answer is that a brief marketplace witness may be the only witness some people ever receive.

Now, think about the rest of your day. Are there people at work that need to know about Jesus? Find your voice for Jesus at work. Listen to the needs of those around you and begin to help them see how the Lord can help. Think about encounters with neighbors and friends. Is it not time for you to speak up for Jesus in every relationship you have? The apostle Paul had this type of witnessing in mind when he wrote, "Let your conversation be always full of grace, seasoned with salt, so that you may know how to answer everyone" (Colossians 4:6 NIV). *Everyone!* Let us stop picking and choosing who we will and will not witness to. Be honest—your "will not witness to" list is much longer, is it not? May we learn to talk about Jesus with everyone. Let us find our voice for Jesus in the marketplaces of our lives.

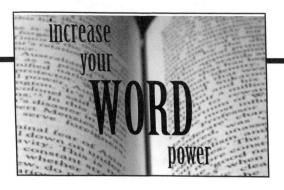
increase your **WORD** power

1 Think about your marketplace. Where do your normal traffic patterns take you? Who are the people that you see on a regular basis? You encounter more people during a day or a week than you probably realize. In prayer, ask God to help you be sensitive to these people and to look for opportunities to share the gospel with them.

2 Romans 5:8 speaks of God's great love demonstrated to us through Jesus' death on the cross. God's love was extended to us even when we were at our worst—while we were yet sinners. Memorize this verse.

3 First Peter 3:18 says, "For Christ died for sins once for all, the righteous for the unrighteous, to bring you to God" (NIV). As you meditate upon what Christ Jesus did in order to bring you into fellowship with God, commit yourself to being present in (not just passing through) your marketplace so that God might draw people to the Savior through your witness.

CHAPTER THIRTEEN
"WE'VE A STORY TO TELL"

Sights, sounds, and smells often conjure up memories of bygone days. I cannot breathe in the aroma of freshly cut grass, wet with the morning dew, without my mind returning to my high school football days when in mid-August we would don our helmets and pads for early morning practices. Likewise, when I hear H. Ernest Nichol's hymn, "We've a Story to Tell," I mentally regress to my sixth year of life. The melody and message of that great missions hymn are indelibly etched upon my memory. I was chosen as a crown bearer for a teenage girl as she had achieved the rank of Acteen Queen (*Acteens* is the missions organization for teenage girls in the Southern Baptist Convention). We marched into the church sanctuary with as much sophistication as possible. The instrumentalists played and the congregation sang these inspiring words:

> We've a story to tell to the nations,
> That shall turn their hearts to the right,
> A story of truth and mercy,
> A story of peace and light,
> A story of peace and light.

For the darkness shall turn to dawning,
And the dawning to noonday bright,
And Christ's great kingdom shall come on earth,
The kingdom of love and light.[31]

That was my first missions experience. Many others would follow over the years, but it all began in that ceremonial rite of passage for a young woman and her six-year-old crown bearer. Not until after my wife and I had surrendered to missionary service did my father remind me that as a nine-year-old boy I had responded to an altar call during Vacation Bible School, indicating an interest in missions. Some memories lay dormant until gentle nudges bring them back to the surface. I can trace a lifetime of influences that leavened my spiritual life until God made his call to missions clear to my mind.

All through college and seminary, a call to missions was in reserve, just out of reach, just beyond a clear understanding. During the 1985 Southern Baptist Convention in Dallas, Texas, as I found my seat for the first session of the annual pastor's conference, God brought it all to the fore. He used a simple promotional brochure, placed on the chairs by the International Mission Board. Taking my seat early, I picked up the pamphlet and began to read. With every word, the conviction grew that God was calling me to be a missionary. I wrestled with this idea briefly, worrying what missionary service would mean for my kids, but earlier that morning I had read Genesis 22 in my Quiet Time. God assured me that if I would release my two boys even as Abraham had been willing to release his hold on his son Isaac, He would take care of them. Arriving home that evening, I mentioned my impressions to my wife. She confirmed similar thoughts and we committed it to prayer. I wrote a letter to the mission board, informing them of our interest. I was not yet fully qualified. I had one semester of seminary remaining and needed another year of ministry experience. By the next spring, however, a candidate consultant from the IMB contacted us and the process of appointment to missionary service moved ahead. On December 6, 1986, Judy and I were officially appointed as missionaries to France. Excitement and anticipation reigned in the Wilson home, for we had a story to tell to the nations, especially to the nation of France.

The story we have to tell the world is a two-part narrative. First, and most importantly, we must tell and retell the story of the life, death, and resurrection of Jesus Christ. Nothing has any meaning apart from His virgin birth, sinless life, miracle-working power, sacrificial death, resurrection from the dead, ascension, and the promise of His return as King of kings and Lord of lords. We tell His story, for only in and through His life and death is there any hope for mankind.

We sing a hymn by Katherine Hankey titled, "I Love to Tell the Story." The second verse resounds with our missionary zeal for evangelism:

> I love to tell the story; 'Tis pleasant to repeat
> What seems each time I tell it, more wonderfully sweet:
> I love to tell the story, for some have never heard
> The message of salvation from God's own holy Word.

I love to tell the story, 'Twill be my theme in glory
To tell the old, old story of Jesus and his love.[32]

I fear that our lives betray our words. We must not really love
to tell the story, for we so seldom do. If we truly believe the story
of salvation, then how can we remain silent? In the book of Acts,
religious and political leaders tried to silence Peter and the other
apostles, but they refused to let their voices be stilled. When
commanded "not to speak or teach at all in the name of Jesus,"
they replied, "we cannot help speaking about what we have seen
and heard" (Acts 4:18-20 NIV). Christ's story had become the
message of their lives. His story was now their story.

Subordinate to His story but essentially intertwined with it is
our story, our testimony. The account of our spiritual journey
toward Jesus and with Jesus is important only because He is who
He claims to be. If His story is less than it is, our story would be
ridiculously insignificant. But since Jesus is indeed Savior and
Lord, our story has meaning and persuasive value. When we
share our personal story of meeting and trusting Jesus, we offer
undeniable evidence of the saving power and forgiveness of
God. Our story builds hope in others who want and need to experience what we have experienced. If God can overcome our sins,
spiritual deficiencies, and weaknesses, then He can do the same
for others. The personal testimony has great power and potential.

Evangelism training materials usually emphasize the sharing
of a personal testimony along with a fuller explanation of God's
plan of salvation. It has always been a convincing way to lead
others to Jesus Christ. The apostle Paul recognized the impor-

tance and pertinence of his own story. Three times in the book of Acts, Paul's testimony is recorded. The first occasion gives us Luke's narrative of his conversion experience on the road to Damascus; the second and third occasions are Paul's own words as he shares his personal story. The third time finds Paul before King Agrippa, who had been consulted about Paul's case after the apostle, fearing extradition, had appealed his case to Caesar. Paul stood before this high-ranking dignitary and proclaimed in confident tones how God had worked in his life. He turned his full attention and persuasive abilities upon Agrippa, who apparently was softening toward the gospel. Paul's testimony was powerfully and mightily used of God to grip ole Agrippa's heart. The invitation hymn "Almost Persuaded" arose from this passage of Scripture which records the response of the king to Paul: "Almost thou persuadest me to be a Christian" (Acts 26:28 KJV). Philip Bliss' hymn reminds us of the danger of putting off a response of faith in Jesus. The third verse says:

"Almost persuaded," harvest is past!
"Almost persuaded," doom comes at last!
"Almost" cannot avail; "Almost" is but to fail!
Sad, sad, that bitter wail—"Almost," but lost![33]

Stopping just short of giving his heart to Jesus, Agrippa arose and declared that Paul was not guilty and could have been released if he had not appealed to Caesar. Regardless of his judicial decision, gospel seed had been planted in the king's life by the personal testimony and witness of Paul.

Most people enjoy talking about themselves. In fact, we rather prefer conversations that center upon ourselves. The personal testimony is a natural way to share our faith and to speak up for Jesus. By declaring what Jesus has done for us, we point people to Him. Our testimonies should be concise and truthful. Few people will listen to your story if you include nonrelevant details and chase uninteresting rabbits. Neither will they remain attentive if it appears your story has become a yarn of legendary proportions. A good testimony briefly summarizes your life before meeting Jesus, the saving encounter you had with Jesus, and what Jesus means to your life today. This was the three-part pattern that Paul used. Several well-constructed sentences in each area could very well be sufficient and prove powerful when shared with others. As an example, allow me to share my brief testimony:

> I was raised by godly parents who loved the Lord and taught me about Jesus. An early childhood experience frightened me severely and caused me to have frequent nightmares. During this turbulent time, my grandmother died, leaving me overcome with a fear of dying. I knew, even at a young age, that if I died without Jesus in my life and heart, I would not go to heaven. A Bible verse that I had memorized in Sunday School helped me to understand that God loved me and had a plan for my life. That verse says, "For God so loved the world that he gave his only begotten

Son, that whosoever believes in him should not perish but have eternal life" (John 3:16). This verse drew me to Jesus and, in prayer, I asked Him to forgive my sin and to live in my heart and life. Since that day, I have never doubted that Jesus answered my prayer of simple, childlike faith. Jesus has been with me, leading my life ever since. Jesus took my sins and my fears away, replacing them with peace and hope. I look forward to living for Jesus for the rest of my life and with Him in heaven.

Having just written these words, I set my stopwatch on my cell phone to see how long it would take for me to say my testimony. Reading slowly and with meaning, it took me 55 seconds to share my testimony. You can learn to recite your testimony even in the brief encounters you have with people throughout the day. Take some time to write out the story of Jesus' work in your life. Mull it over in your mind. Rework it until you are comfortable with its wording and flow. Then speak up and tell your story. You truly have a story to tell!

Mission volunteers who travel to foreign fields of service are at a disadvantage. They desire to witness and minister, but barriers of language prevent them from communicating, except through interpreters. To facilitate the sharing of testimonies, I asked one group of volunteers to write out their testimonies and mail them to me a month prior to their arrival. I then translated their words into French and made numerous copies. The plan was to present a written testimony to those we met on the streets and in homes. In written form, their stories could be read and re-read, perhaps having an even greater affect.

With the process of translation complete and copies made, the volunteers arrived and we ventured out into the streets. At first, one of the volunteers was very eager to distribute his half-sheet printed testimony, but as person after person refused to take his handout, he grew frustrated and discouraged. Those who did not accept a copy did so with a strange look upon their faces. It was not the handout that turned them off, for the French are used to having flyers of all kinds shoved in their faces as they come out of subway stations. The problem that caused such con-sternated looks was what the well-intentioned volunteer was say-ing—or at least trying to say. I could not help but laugh when I realized what he was doing. As he handed a person his printed testimony, he would point at it and say, "Moy, moy." The French had no idea what he meant. Of course, he was giving an English pronunciation to the French personal pronoun for "me," which is spelled *moi* but pronounced *mwa*. He wanted people to know that the handout was his story.

Nearly everyone loves a good story. I can remember stories my mother told me at bedtime many years ago. She is a reader. I imagine she has read thousands of novels. Stories captivate our attention and preoccupy our minds. If we are watching a story unfold on television, we generally scream at the TV set if those three hated words appear on the screen—"To Be Continued." Calvin Miller underscores the importance of story in his book, *Spirit, Word and Story*: "We all have a fondness for stories. We are storytellers, story hearers, and, indeed, story writers."[34] With his usual flair he sums it up in the statement, "Life is as warm as a bedtime story."[35]

Our stories of faith need that warmth and tenderness. Testimonies should be more than dates and facts. Real emotion fueled the living out of our experiences; we must, therefore, retell them with passion. I do not necessarily mean that we ought to tell our stories with tears flowing down our cheeks but rather that we must make them come alive in the minds of those who hear us. Have you ever heard a work colleague tell the story of his recent vacation, white-water rafting in Colorado? He speaks with enthusiasm and passion, reliving the rapids as he speaks. You can almost feel the cold water splash up on your face. You sense the danger and adrenaline rush. You think, "Wow! What an experience. Wish I could know that kind of thrill and joy!"

When you talk about the moment of your salvation from sin and eternal separation from God, do you speak with passion? What Jesus has done for you is more exciting and more danger-ous than any rafting trip. Our goal, of course, is not to draw attention to ourselves but to the Lord who saved us and walks with us. Our stories should make Jesus the central character. Our struggles and experiences are the setting for the great act of sal-vation wrought by God through Christ's death on the cross. We must portray Him in such a way that people are attracted to Him. This story is a dynamic and living account of our relationship with Jesus. We are called to be gospel storytellers, and according to Calvin Miller, "storytellers are glorious participants in and the explainers of the narrative of God's revelation. We are called to bring the Bible story to bear on the life stories"[36] of others.

Think back to the last sermon you heard. If you remember anything about it, it is probably not the Scripture passage exegeted by your pastor or the points of his outline. What is memorable is some story told in the midst of the message—an illustration that made you laugh or some heart wrenching account that brought tears to your eyes and a lump to your throat. Miller insists "that stories are the real life changers. . . . They confront and change lives."[37] God has called you to the life-changing ministry of telling your story.

Your story need not be long or complicated. Scriptural examples of telling one's story include the man born blind (John 9). When asked about what happened, he simply stated, "I was blind but now I see!" The religious authorities were arguing about whether Jesus had the authority, the right, or the power to do what He did. The healed man just told the truth about what Jesus had done for him and gave God all the glory. A life had been transformed; blinded eyes now saw the light of day, and a story of faith had begun. I wonder how many times that man, born blind but now seeing, told and retold his story. Indeed, we have a story to tell to the nations. If we tell it simply but with passion, people will listen. Some will respond to the Savior and begin to share their own story of faith.

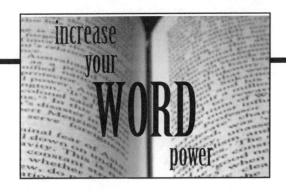

1 Read Paul's personal testimony in Acts 22:3-21 and Acts 26:4-23. You will notice that Paul spoke of his life before knowing Jesus, how he came to know Jesus, and how Jesus changed his life. You have a similar story. The details are different but the outline is the same. Write two or three sentences for each of these points:

My life before knowing Jesus:

_____

_____

_____

_____

_____

How I came to know Jesus:

_____

_____

_____

_____

_____

_____

How Jesus changed my life:

_____

_____

_____

_____

_____

2 Re-work these sentences, adding others if necessary, until you are satisfied that you have a concise statement of your personal spiritual journey to and with Jesus. Practice saying your testimony to a family member or church member. Pray, then go share your testimony with some lost person. You can introduce your testimony with a question like: Can I share with you the most important thing that ever happened to me?

CHAPTER FOURTEEN

GRUMBLING THE GOSPEL

People are listening. They hear what we say and how we say it. No, our houses and cars are not bugged. Our neighbors most likely do not utilize high-tech listening devices to eavesdrop on our personal lives. Some neighbors may indeed be nosy, but people in general do pay attention to what transpires around them.

The ancient Hebrews believed that words had an independent existence after being spoken. Blessings and cursings spoken upon people in the Old Testament carried incredible weight for just this reason. Once a word was spoken, it had a continuing operative force to affect lives. There is much truth in this concept of the power of words. If you have ever spoken an ill-advised or ill-timed word in anger or scorn, you know the lasting impact your words have on the people to whom you speak.

The church my father pastored when I was a child had a big blue church bus. I rode to church with my parents, so I never rode the big blue bus, but I wanted to. I thought it would be fun to ride with a friend of mine one Sunday when I was about twelve years old. He was a church friend who lived in a different school district. I had never been to his house before. Of course, there were others on the bus. One by one, and sometimes two by two, my fellow riders were dropped off at their homes. When the bus was nearly empty, it stopped in front of a very small and neglected house. With my sharp intellect, I deduced this was the house of my friend. We had been teasing and cutting up during the entire ride, and I jumped at the chance to get in one last parting shot. "Who lives there? Who lives in that house? That can't be your house, it's awful," I exclaimed in jest, giving my friend a gentle push toward the exit. Only, he did not get out of the bus. It was not his stop; it was not his house. Two sisters made their way toward the open door, heads hung low in shame, and got off the bus. They did not look back as they hurried to the front door of their humble home. The door shut behind them and I never saw them again. They never got back on that bus. They never returned to church. My words, though not intentionally aimed at them, had insensitively crushed their spirits. The pastor's son had ridiculed their very existence. They probably never knew how ashamed I was or that I am haunted by my actions even to this day. My words, once spoken, came alive and continued to exert their harmful force.

Jesus took words very seriously. He never spoke without thinking, never used words in retaliation or vengeance, never failed to measure his words and speak appropriately. The apostle Peter, on the other hand, was the exact opposite. He often spoke without the synapses of his brain connecting. He used words to argue and to question and to deny his Lord. Peter understood the difference between Jesus and himself, for it is Peter who writes of Jesus, "He committed no sin, and no deceit was found in his mouth. When they hurled their insults at him, he did not retaliate; when he suffered, he made no threats" (1 Peter 2:22-23 NIV).

Jesus understood the import of words and their potential danger if not used correctly. "For out of the overflow of the heart the mouth speaks," He taught. "But I tell you that men will have to give account on the day of judgment for every careless word they have spoken. For by your words you will be acquitted, and by your words you will be condemned" (Matthew 12:34, 36-37 NIV). It is not very comforting to know that a record of our words is being kept until judgment. More frightening yet is the prospect that a record of our silences—those times we had opportunity to witness but did not—is also being recorded.

If the negative impact of words persists over time, then we may also conclude that words spoken to edify and encourage also have an enduring effect. When we speak for Jesus and sow gospel seed into the lives of people, we should rejoice that God can cause that seed to germinate, take root, and grow. What this means is that we must be careful to speak only that which promotes faith and draws minds and hearts closer to Jesus. One negative word or conversation has the power to nullify many positive words.

Jacqueline was a middle-aged woman who had been on a long spiritual journey in search of Jesus. Years of skepticism and doubt had caused her to reject the basic message of the Bible, but then her husband fell ill. Cancer invaded his body and unleashed its horrors upon him. He suffered terribly, but the illness led him and his wife to reevaluate their position on spiritual matters. They became seekers and began attending home Bible studies and church worship services. The gospel took root in their hearts and they both placed their faith in Jesus Christ. Just before his death, Jacqueline's husband was baptized in the hospital. After a time of mourning, she too submitted herself to that act of obedience.

Now, as a baptized believer, she had begun another, perhaps even more difficult journey—a journey of faith and striving toward Christlikeness. Through her grief and heartache, she became very active in all the church was doing. Her faith was growing. One Sunday, during our praise and worship time (most French Baptist churches had a brief time during the worship service in which people were free to suggest a hymn, read a poem or Scripture, sing a chorus, pray, etc.), Jacqueline gathered her courage and began to pray out loud for the first time ever in public. I knew how hard it was for her, for we had discussed her reservations about public prayer on numerous occasions. In the middle of her prayer, disaster struck. She was interrupted by the unintelligible voice of a woman speaking in tongues. Jacqueline fell silent as she listened to that which she could not understand. It was a short message, followed by silence. Then the unthinkable happened—the woman who had spoken in tongues interpreted her own message. The interpretation was a message given in the singular form of the French word for repentance: "You repent!"

Jacqueline was convinced the message was a word from God directed toward her. She was crushed and demoralized, asking, "Why is God so upset with me?" I remained at the church for three hours that afternoon, counseling with her and offering her comfort, but the damage had been done. Words spoken out of spiritual arrogance and ignorance had wounded irreparably a young and immature believer. The gift of tongues had been abused and misused by the devil to disrupt and destroy. Language has power both for good and evil.

The church ought to be the one place where words bless rather than curse, but sadly that is not the case. Hurtful and hateful words are often heard when the church is gathered. Church members all too often use words to speak curses upon fellow believers. These harmful words between Christians spill over into the communities in which we live. Do not be surprised if the town's people know all about what the church is squabbling over. Lost people laugh at us and rationalize their absence from church gatherings by pointing out the hypocrisy of our lives and words. No wonder the apostle Paul took great pains to warn believers about the misuse of words:

> Do not let any unwholesome talk come out of
> your mouths, but only what is helpful for build-
> ing others up according to their needs, that it
> may benefit those who listen. And do not grieve
> the Holy Spirit of God, with whom you were
> sealed for the day of redemption. Get rid of all
> bitterness, rage and anger, brawling and slander,
> along with every form of malice. Be kind and
> compassionate to one another, forgiving each
> other, just as in Christ God forgave you
> (Ephesians 4:29-32 NIV).

James elaborates the same theme in his epistle:

> We all stumble in many ways. If anyone is never
> at fault in what he says, he is a perfect man, able
> to keep his whole body in check. When we put
> bits into the mouths of horses to make them obey
> us, we can turn the whole animal. Or take ships as
> an example. Although they are so large and are
> driven by strong winds, they are steered by a very
> small rudder wherever the pilot wants to go.
> Likewise the tongue is a small part of the body,
> but it makes great boasts. Consider what a great
> forest is set on fire by a small spark. The tongue
> also is a fire, a world of evil among the parts of
> the body. It corrupts the whole person, sets the
> whole course of his life on fire, and is itself set on
> fire by hell. All kinds of animals, birds, reptiles
> and creatures of the sea are being tamed and have
> been tamed by man, but no man can tame the
> tongue. It is a restless evil, full of deadly poison.
> With the tongue we praise our Lord and Father,
> and with it we curse men, who have been made in
> God's likeness. Out of the same mouth come
> praise and cursing. My brothers, this should not
> be (James 3:2-10 NIV).

Given the impact of words, we need to understand that we
are always bearing some type of witness. Our words may testify

to our faith in Jesus or they may detract from it. Since our witness is accomplished primarily through words, every word we speak is part of the message we convey. Not only must we purposefully speak about Jesus in intentional witnessing situations, but we must also take great care that every word spoken, in whatever situation, does not disparage the gospel.

For example, Don attends the weeknight visitation program of his church. Together with two other individuals, he knocks on the door of Ed Smith, who welcomes them cordially and listens to them present the gospel. Ed has attended church several times but has numerous questions and hesitations. He puts off a decision for Christ that night, but indicates he would like to talk about it again. On Friday morning, however, Ed goes into a local café for a light breakfast and coffee. He overhears a conversation at the booth behind him and recognizes Don's voice. He leans back and listens as the four individuals, all members of Don's church, share the latest criticism about their young pastor. The conversation then turns to the beautiful divorcée who just moved into town. Ed is shocked by the suggestive comments coming from Don's mouth. Ed does not make his presence known to Don and the others as he leaves the restaurant. Several weeks later, Don knocks on Ed's door to continue their spiritual conversation, but Ed refuses to let him in. Don wonders why Ed has quit coming to church and concludes that Ed is just too hard-hearted to trust the Lord as Savior. Ed must be a hopeless case. Sadly, Don's negative words far outweigh his words of witness.

If the truth be known, we spend far more time grumbling the gospel than we do presenting the gospel. By "grumbling the gospel" I mean letting our words and conversations deteriorate to the world's level. Our complaints, grievances, and grumblings, when expressed verbally, present a view of the gospel that unchurched people take to heart. Many of the obstacles that keep lost people from accepting Jesus are obstacles that we ourselves have placed in their way. Even when we do not think we are bearing witness, we are, in fact, witnessing, often more power-fully than we can imagine. When we grumble the gospel we are distorting the truth and betraying our Lord. The Bible teaches that love is one of the leading characteristics of the Lord and His people, but when we say and do unloving things we are putting forth a false impression of who Jesus is and who we are sup-posed to be. Our words deny and often disown the very Jesus we want to present to the lost. The discrepancy between our words spoken intentionally in witness encounters and our casual words of everyday life is obvious and gives evidence of our hypocrisy. People are listening. Is it any wonder they question what they hear and doubt that there is any truth to the gospel we proclaim?

Of necessity, we must admit that indeed we are all hyp-ocrites. Not one of us is able to keep life and belief perfectly lined up. We often falter on the side of improper actions that lead the lost around us to ridicule our faith because we are inconsis-tent and do not apply the teachings we proclaim to our own lives. To counter this obvious imbalance, our witness should be con-fessional. We have not yet arrived (see Philippians 3:7-14) and we must convey to those around us that we are still on the pil-grimage we are inviting them to begin. We do not come to the lost as if we do not face the same struggles, temptations, and trials they face. We come alongside them as fellow strugglers, yet because we have placed our trust in Jesus, we have spiritual resources that enable us to bear up under the load. This is the power of life transformation that the Holy Spirit is working into our lives. As He transforms us, we have His strength to stand in His truth and to share that truth unashamedly with the lost. Our witness becomes a powerful testimony of God's ability and desire to transform lives. If He has saved me, He can save you. If He can use me in spite of my failures and even my hypocrisies, then He can use you. We tend to begin grumbling the gospel when we lose sight of this life transforming work of the Spirit of God. A person who is aware of how far God has brought him usually does not struggle with keeping a positive outlook on his daily life. Those who grumble have lost sight of God's amazing work of grace in their lives. This is the point, after all. We are called to witness to the saving grace of God. He offers forgiveness to those who do not deserve to be forgiven. He extends mercy to those lost in sin. Knowing this, how could we do anything but witness?

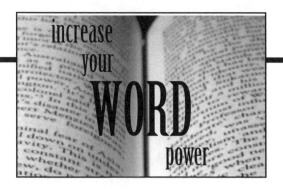

increase your WORD power

1 Ephesians 1:7 proclaims, "In him we have redemption through his blood, the forgiveness of our trespasses, according to the riches of his grace." Think of the extent of God's forgiveness extended to you. All your sinful thoughts, words, actions, motives, etc. are covered by the blood of Jesus. Can you remember the joy and inner peace you experienced when you first trusted Jesus? Pause and thank God for saving you from your sins.

2 Reflect upon the conversations you had in the last twenty-four hours. Did your words magnify Jesus? Did your words edify others? Did your words criticize? Were your words harmful? Were you conscience of the need to bear witness to Christ at all times?

3 Are there people to whom you need to go with a sincere apology for the way you talked to them? When things are not going well at work, do you lash out? Do you join in the course, raucous joking of others? Do you demean others? Do you have a critical spirit? Pray, asking God to forgive you these sins. Ask Him to help you use your spoken words to edify, encourage, and witness.

CHAPTER FIFTEEN

THAT ALL THE WORLD MAY HEAR

One of the best soulwinners I know does not know she is a soulwinner. In fact, if I mentioned it to her, she would probably laugh out loud and deny the charge. I would not dare mention this to her for fear that she would be intimidated and stop doing what she is doing. She is not typical; she succeeds in winning people while others make weak and futile attempts, if any attempt at all.

Lori does not attend the church's Tuesday-evening evangelism training. She does not know any memorized evangelistic presentation. She really does not know how to witness in any conventional way. She is not a part of any program of evangelism training or outreach. She is not a Bible scholar. What is her secret? She has lost friends and she wants them to be saved. Most Christians do not have a burden for the lost and do not know how to witness. Some know how to witness but do not have a burden for lost people. There are a few who may not know how to witness but, because of their deep burden, witness in spite of themselves.

More people have come into the church through this one woman than through any one else. Her approach? She takes it one person or one family at a time and stays with it until they gladly receive the Lord. She has discovered or rediscovered the biblical principle of investing her life into the lives of others. Robert Coleman recognizes that this investment of life was the method of Jesus with his apostles.[38] As Jesus *associated* with His followers, He led them to saving faith and developed them into reproducing believers. Lori is willing to give of herself and her time to those who need the Lord. She does it by being a friend and doing what friends do—but with a different goal in mind. She does not view the friend as a means to her own fulfillment or to meet some need in her own life. She truly wants that friend to know the Lord.

Lori's heart for lost friends is best exemplified by what happened just a few years ago. She had a childhood friend for whom she had been praying for most of her life. This friend had taken a path through life that brought her much anguish and turmoil. Lori remained steadfast through the years, encouraging her friend to turn to the Lord. Only after much heartache and many years did this friend finally give her heart to Jesus. Lori was radiant as her beloved friend was baptized. What happened next was disheartening to those who knew Lori. A couple of women in the church befriended Lori's friend. Soon she was spending all her time with them, forsaking her friendship with Lori. She even gave credit to these new friends for helping her come to Jesus. Lori, however, did not complain or feel threatened. She was content to see her friend in church. Her love for friend and Savior was such that what mattered most to her was not her personal need but the salvation of one who had previously been lost. Hers was a selfless love and a sacrificial desire to see her friend saved.

Churches need more members like Lori. Most churches are not blessed with soulwinners—believers who go out witnessing to anybody and everybody. Most American churches believe that evangelism is the pastor's duty. They pay him to do the dirty work of witnessing. It is my firm belief, though, that believers who are firmly committed to being personal witnesses do exist. We just have trouble identifying them. We want these soulwinners to fit into our mold. We want them to lead out on the weeknight visitation program. We have so pressed evangelism into a specific package that we limit the Spirit's working in other, more effective ways. We want witnessing to be neatly contained into time slots that we can manage. We set apart a couple of hours one night a week and expect the Holy Spirit to show up and work miracles of grace upon people with whom we have little or no contact and for whom we have no concern at other times. How can we be so concerned for their souls on Tuesday night but not think about them again until the next week if they are not home? I wonder if the people we are trying to reach see through us and understand that they are trophies to be won and shown off at the next church service.

Not long ago, a deacon and I went to visit a man for whom we had been praying. He attended Sunday worship services regularly, but he had not made a profession of faith. Several men in the church had witnessed to him on different occasions. He was outside in his driveway when we drove up. He greeted us and we talked casually for a couple of minutes. Then he turned the subject to church matters, stating, "Well, I guess you're here because you want me to come down front at church and be baptized." I think he saw himself as a prize to be won. I told him that was not the reason for my visit. My desire was to help him see his need for the Savior so that he would give his life totally and freely to Jesus. He was surprised by my response. I believe that if I had agreed with him, he would have been willing to go through the motions of "joining" the church, but he would not have truly been saved. Once he understood that I was talking about an entirely different level of decision, he quickly let me know that he felt no need for the Lord. His life was good and he had no needs. For nearly two years this man continued to attend our worship services without showing much outward interest in accepting Christ for himself. Then something changed—his sons went to summer church camp and accepted Christ during a service there. He escorted his sons to the front of the church to declare their profession of faith and told me that he was ready to commit his life to the Lord as well. I had the great joy of baptizing him, knowing that he was not just going through the motions.

Those who do make professions of faith and follow the Lord in baptism often complain soon afterward that they are being ignored by those who wanted so desperately to see them saved. In our evangelistic zeal, we often leave the newly converted unattended as we go off in search of more converts. Is it any wonder that many new believers find the transition to living the Christian life hard and that most never become active witnesses? No one shows them how. These pitfalls are prevalent for the simple reason that we see evangelism as a program of the church rather than a personal lifestyle. We witness at set times and to set people (those determined to be good prospects for our church).

We will never see a great turning of souls to the Lord if we only witness when it is convenient to us or when we can squeeze it into a fixed timeslot. We will not see many saved if we give evangelism only minimal attention and time.

How much time is necessary to lead a person to faith in Jesus? As much time as that person requires. It varies with each person, but this is not the right question. What we should be asking is this: How much time am I willing to invest into the spiritual life of some lost friend? The cost is great, because time is a precious commodity. We waste countless hours doing things of no eternal value: we watch TV shows with no intrinsic worth; read books with no spiritual significance; play games that edify no one; chat online into the wee hours of the morning—but we jealously guard what little free time we have left over after doing these meaningless activities. We resent the implication that our time could be better spent. We boast of our busy schedules as if they prove our worth as persons, but we do not realize that our busy-ness keeps us from matters of real value. Most believers, if asked and if honest, would say they are too busy to be involved in any kind of witnessing activity. They are wrong on two fronts. First, they have more free time than they think they do; they just need to reprioritize their activities. Second, the claim to be too busy to witness reveals their belief that witnessing takes place only at a set, programmed time. While they may not get home from work in time to attend a weekday outreach program, they certainly can speak of Jesus throughout the day. If they would approach witnessing as a lifestyle, they would find ample time to talk to others about Jesus.

Not only do we tend to misappropriate our time, but, in general, churches do not plan for evangelistic growth. Put a bit differently, we plan to fail or, at least, we do not plan for the explosive growth that is possible if God's people were witnessing as they ought. If we evangelized like Lori, mentioned at the beginning of this chapter, we could not contain the growth. Our buildings would be too small. Currently, I am pastor of a church that averages just about 170 in Sunday School and 210 in Worship. If each attending member would invest his or her life into the life of an unchurched person throughout the next year, and if only one third of those persons began attending, then we would be out of space completely in less than two years. Churches just are not prepared to receive that many additional people and, quite honestly, most have no plans in place to grow to that extent. One church I pastored was led by my predecessor to build a new building on the edge of town. Their "vision" included a downsizing of educational space. The old building had twenty-four Sunday School classrooms available for use; the new building only had eighteen. The church had not planned to grow at all.

We are content with our one or two hours of witnessing on a given weekday evening, but this yields little if any results. We have planned to fail. We proclaim our missionary and evangelistic zeal with great pride—"That all the world may know." But our zeal amounts to empty rhetoric. It is easy to talk about the world because it has no face, no personality, and requires no time. It is beyond us and we cannot touch it. The church speaks too much in generalities. Our comfort zone will not allow us to get personal. In his book, *Soul Survivor*, Philip Yancey dedicates a chapter each to thirteen individuals (his spiritual directors or mentors) who have transformed his life by their writings and experiences. Explaining the influence of Robert Coles, Yancey writes, "Comfortable people, he [Coles] noticed, were apt to have a stunted sense of compassion, more likely to love humanity in general but less likely to love one person in particular."[39] If we are serious about reaching our world for Jesus, then we had better start with the face, the personality, and the person that is right in front of us. The only way to win the world is one person at a time.

Somehow, Lori learned this secret and is living it out. Unknown to her, she has rediscovered the only method of evangelism that is truly effective—she loves people to the Lord. I am not insinuating that mass evangelism efforts are ineffective. Millions have been won to Christ through this approach. Even so, many who attend these types of rallies have been invited by someone who cares for their soul. In his research, Thom Rainer found that one of the leading factors in influencing the unchurched to come to faith in the Lord is a personal relationship with a Christian, most likely a family member or friend. Over one half of those involved in his study indicated that "someone from the church they joined shared Christ with them," leaving "little doubt as to the importance of personal evangelism in reaching the unchurched."[40] Unfortunately, Rainer's research also reveals that "only one person is reached for Christ for every eighty-five church members in America."[41] The evidence of our love is the time we are willing to give to leading the lost to Jesus. If one person can lead a friend to Jesus by a commitment of time and witness, what are the other eighty-four doing? Most Christians are not witnessing: if they were, the ratio of church members to converts would be much lower. Rainer identifies an "effective evangelistic church" as one that has "at least twenty-six conversions per year and a conversion ratio of less than 20:1."[42]

I have in my personal library some of my father's old books. Some of these were published by the Southern Baptist Convention for the purpose of training and encouraging church members in evangelism. Back then, the SBC liked to emphasize growth goal slogans. One of these slogans, put out in booklet form, was "Two Win One." This campaign marked the centennial celebration of the SBC. The booklet is a series of articles by prominent church and convention leaders. A chart indicates a national conversion ratio of 25.66 to one. The goal of the campaign was to reduce that ratio to 2:1, but an article by C. E. Bryant states, "Do we as Christians not know a truth immeasurable in its meaning and significance, and worth telling to all we meet? Each win one."[43] By 1953 the national ratio had declined to 20:1, but leaders were not satisfied with this number. The Convention adopted another campaign: "A million more in '54."[44] To promote this emphasis, J. N. Barnette suggested a conversion ratio of one baptism for every eight members. He writes,

> *One to Eight* represents a degree of success in evangelism which should be realized, on the average, by Southern Baptist churches—that is, year by

year we should be able to report one baptism for every eight church members. At present the record shows approximately one baptism for every twenty church members. This ratio of baptisms to church members has remained about the same for our Convention as a whole for many years. Growing numbers of churches, however, have increased their baptisms to a great degree—many of them baptizing people at the rate of one for every ten, eight, six, five, and even two church members.[45]

This goal was not quite achieved, but the vision is exciting. Today, we are ten times worse in winning people to Christ. Should it take eighty-five of us to lead one soul to Christ? Are you doing your part?

Let me give you several ideas that you can use over the next year to lead some friend or neighbor to Christ. Now, mind you, these ideas will not come easy or yield quick results. Putting them into practice will cost you valuable time, but it is time invested in the spiritual life of a soul precious to God.

Get to know the person as well as he or she will allow. Never press for more information than the person is willing to give. You must be a good listener. We err in thinking that witnessing is merely us talking and them listening (see Chapter Seven). Ask for and listen to their story. Ask questions and seek to understand their life's journey. Do not minimize any emotion or hurt they have suffered. Do not overcorrect misunderstandings of the church—in time the Lord will put things in perspective for them. The key here is relationship. Build an honest friendship based on mutual respect. Let your genuine concern for their well-being be evident. Love them in spite of flaws and sins.

Lest you think I am advocating a form of lifestyle evangelism (witnessing by action rather than by voice), let me encourage you to be open and up-front about your commitment to Jesus Christ. Your lifestyle ought to be one of verbal witnessing. Many evangelistic opportunities are missed because we skirt the central issue of our faith. We water down our discipleship for fear it might scare off someone. When we finally bring up the issue of faith, it seems incongruent with the way we have been previously presenting ourselves. "Oh, by the way, I'm a Christian," spoken weeks or months into a friendship will appear dishonest and will minimize how important our faith really is to us. Those you are trying to win to Christ ought to see Jesus in you and hear Jesus from you.

Invite your friends to church services often. Do not be put off by them declining your invitations. I had not been on my first pastorate church field long when the Director of Missions stopped by for a visit. In the midst of our conversation about reaching people for Jesus, he encouraged me to keep at it no matter what the response I might receive. He shared a statistic that he had gleaned from some SBC study that indicated that on average it is necessary to make seventeen contacts with a person before they will attend your church. I know Christians who have invited a loved one for years before the person finally attended church with them. Others may attend the first time you ask. We might just be surprised to know how many may indeed attend with that first simple invitation. Do not pressure people to attend. Do not make the invitation an all or nothing issue. Thinking that your friend is getting irritated by your persistent invitations, you may want to say, "I am going to ask you just one more time. If you refuse, then I will leave you alone." Don't. The person may be under deep conviction of sin, but may jump at the opportunity to get us to stop speaking of spiritual things. If a person does not accept your invitation, do not write off him or her. Faithfully invite the person over and over again.

Socialize with your friend. Enjoy each other's presence. Introduce them to other Christians. Let them introduce you to their lost friends. This is what the apostle Matthew did after he left his tax collector's booth to follow Jesus. Evidently, he threw a party and invited all his "sinner" friends and associates to come. He also invited Jesus (see Mark 2:14-17). Think of the impact of Jesus at that gathering—laughing, eating, and rejoicing with one who had turned from his sin by faith, drawing others like Matthew to himself. Think what your presence in the midst of a gathering of such people might mean for their understanding of what it means to follow Jesus. It is helpful for those without Christ to see believers interacting with them in a normal way. More than that, it is quite helpful if they see you dealing with the same issues and problems that they deal with. They will notice that you are handling them differently because of your faith. Let your life be transparent. When you put on masks for different occasions, people will not see Jesus in you and you will not speak of him for fear that your mask might slip off. When you are transparent, people can see Jesus through you and your words spoken in witness ring true.

The greatest and best witnessing tool is one that is often overlooked—the Bible. As you develop a relationship with a lost person, ask if he would like to read the Bible together. Once a week, you could meet over coffee and read a chapter of the Gospel of John, for example. Do not use this time to preach or condemn. Let it be a time of introduction to and interaction with God's Word. The Holy Spirit will speak through the words of Scripture. Indeed, the Bible says, "Faith cometh by hearing, and hearing by the word of God" (Romans 10:17 KJV). As you read together, pray that your friend will "believe that Jesus is the Christ, the Son of God" (John 20:31). This is the stated purpose of the Gospel of John. He wrote it as an evangelistic tool. The frequency of your meetings together will depend on your friend's willingness and your commitment of time. Getting together once a week to read a chapter or two may be a good starting point.

If believers would set apart an hour a week to read Scripture with some lost friend, I am convinced that God would use it to draw many to the Savior. Again, this would demand an investment of time and energy and would require you to be more familiar with the Bible. You would need to be ready to answer questions that may be asked. These may be simple questions about a story from the life of Jesus or profound theological questions about the nature of God. There is no shame in saying, "I'm not sure how to answer your question, but I will find out and get back to you."

If you begin this process of reading Scripture together, then see it through. If you agree together to read the Gospel of John, then by all means read the Gospel of John. You might be surprised how many will willingly place their faith in Jesus by the end of the book. It is important, after their conversion, to continue the practice of reading together, helping them to grow as a new believer.

Above all, pray for the salvation of your friend. Ask God to use your love and friendship to draw her to Jesus. One by one, love people to Jesus so that one by one the whole world may know Him.

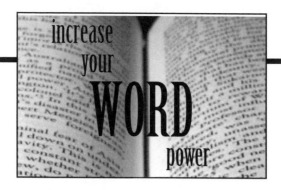

increase your WORD power

1 Using Thom Rainer's analysis of an effective evangelistic church (at least 26 conversions per year and a member to baptism ratio of 20:1), how does the church you attend measure up? Are you doing your part?

2 Read Romans 10:9-13. Twice in these verses, God says He will save. That is God's part in the process. Our part is found in verses 14-15. The question comes to us: How will they hear if we are silent?

3 Are you willing to commit yourself—your time and energy—so that one person can come to know Jesus during the next year? Pray about how you can reprioritize your use of time so that you can invest it into the life of someone who needs Jesus.

CHAPTER SIXTEEN

THE MARTYRS' CRY

Ask an average Christian why he or she does not go out on church visitation and you are likely to get this response: "I am afraid someone will slam the door in my face." In over twenty-five years of ministry and witnessing, I have never once had a door slammed in my face. I have had some doors closed quickly and some unfriendly words said to me, but slammed doors are a rarity. Yet, the fear of some verbal or physical rejection keeps many believers at home on visitation night. Worse, it silences their voice of witness. Of course, I am talking about Christians in America, where freedom of speech is interpreted by many followers of Jesus to mean the freedom to be silent if they wish. God has never given us the option of silence. To be a follower of Jesus is a call to speak—to raise our voices in witness.

The scenario is different on the other side of the globe. Christians in some countries are forbidden to speak in the name of Jesus, yet without hesitation and refusing to fear the consequences, they speak boldly for the Lord. Even the threat of death, imposed if they are caught evangelizing, does not deter them. They may take steps to be more careful, but they would not even consider silence as an option.

Interestingly, the New Testament word for witness is the Greek word *martyr*. A witness gives testimony of things he has experienced. In common usage today, the word refers to suffering and, ultimately, death due to one's beliefs. Over the centuries, to be a witness for Jesus became associated with giving one's life for the cause of Jesus. Alvin Reid writes, "Many early believers died because of their commitment to Christ, leading to the expression *martyr* to describe such faithful witnesses. For many early Christians, it was better to die than to stop testifying about Christ."[46]

In the book of Acts, especially, we see how witnessing aroused deep emotions and caused hostile reactions. The name of Jesus brought out the best and the worst in people. As early as the Day of Pentecost, derogatory remarks were heaped upon those who witnessed in the power of the indwelling Spirit. They were accused of being drunk—so exuberant was their witness. Not long thereafter, the apostles John and Peter were arrested for healing a man and speaking in Jesus' name. The authorities could not deny the healing, for the man stood there before them. They turned their hateful remarks on the apostles' testimony of the healing, forbidding them to speak in the name of Jesus (Acts 4:18).

Upon their release, however, they returned to a gathering of believers and prayed for courage to witness amidst such hostility: "Now, Lord, consider their threats and enable your servants to speak your word with great boldness" (Acts 4:29 NIV). God responded powerfully to such praying: "And when they had prayed, the place where they had gathered together was shaken, and they were all filled with the Holy Spirit and began to speak the word of God with boldness" (Acts 4:31).

Again, in Acts 5, the apostles were arrested and put in jail. They were warned about speaking in the name of Jesus and then they were flogged. Let us not pass by this point too quickly. Floggings were extremely brutal and often caused death. Nonetheless, the apostles survived and rejoiced "because they had been counted worthy of suffering disgrace for the Name" (Acts 5:41 NIV). Stephen, one of the seven men chosen by the church to assist the apostles, spoke out so boldly about Jesus that he was dragged outside of town and stoned to death. From that moment, "a great persecution broke out against the church" (Acts 8:1 NIV).

Acts 5 and 8 provide a very remarkable contrast. In response to their arrest and being ordered not to speak anymore in the name of Jesus, the apostles intensified their witnessing, going "from *house to house* . . . teaching and proclaiming the good news" of Jesus (see Acts 5:42 NIV, italics added). The outcome of their intensified witnessing was intensified persecution: "But Saul began ravaging the church, entering *house after house*, and dragging off men and women, he would put them in prison" (Acts 8:3, italics added). The result of this fiercer persecution was that the believers were scattered to the surrounding areas. As they left Jerusalem, they took the gospel of Jesus with them and "went about preaching the word" (Acts 8:4). The word used here for "preaching" is the word *evangelizing*. Though persecuted, they evangelized all the more—not just house to house, but now region to region. Persecution does not and will not stop the spread of the gospel. Where there is persecution, you will always find bold witnesses. What interrupts the spread of the gospel is a desire for safety and personal security. In America, with no threat of outward persecution, we have ceased to go door to door. In fact, many church leaders are advocating that we find a different approach. Many claim that going house to house is no longer a valid method of evangelism. We have adopted a "Ya'll come" mentality. Rather than going after the lost, we sit back and wait for the lost to come to us.

The apostle Paul, before his conversion on the road to Damascus, was the instigator of much of the persecution that broke out upon the first Christians. God had a different purpose for his life and sent Ananias to confirm Paul in his newfound faith, saying, "This man is my chosen instrument to carry my name before the Gentiles and their kings and before the people of Israel. I will show him how much he must suffer for my name" (Acts 9:15-16 NIV). This suffering was not some sort of punishment for his role in the persecution against God's people; it just went with the territory. Paul was to be a witness to the nations. Wherever he went, persecution was on his heels. For Paul, witnessing always resulted in opposition. Of course, in spite of fierce opposition, thousands of people were saved through Paul's witness. Persecution often fans the flames of revival. In the course of the spread of the Christian faith, the death of James added fuel to that fire. The same fate awaited Peter, but an angel of the Lord delivered him miraculously (Acts 12).

By the end of the book, Paul was in prison, yet the gospel was being proclaimed "boldly and without hindrance" (Acts

28:31 NIV). Paul reviews his various persecutions, mentioning labors, imprisonments, beatings, scourgings, stonings, and all sorts of dangers (2 Corinthians 11:23-27).

It is no wonder that Paul writes, "In fact, everyone who wants to live a godly life in Christ Jesus will be persecuted" (2 Timothy 3:12 NIV). He was building upon what Jesus had already taught:

> If the world hates you, you know that it has hated me before it hated you. If you were of the world, the world would love its own; but because you are not of the world, but I chose you out of the world, because of this the world hates you. Remember the word that I said to you, 'A slave is not greater than his master.' If they persecuted me, they will also persecute you; if they kept my word, they will keep yours also. But these things they will do to you for my name's sake, because they do not know the One who sent me (John 15:18-21).

These words seem odd to us. In this country, we have no fear of violent reaction to our witness. Although there are some signs that this may be changing, we currently have no fear of persecution. Yet, these words ring loud and clear for many believers in the world. Alvin Reid adds, "The reason many believers today do not attempt to share their faith is because they have gotten over their salvation! The early believers did not—indeed they could not—get past the radical transformation they experienced through the gospel."[47] In the introduction to her book, *In the Lion's Den*, Nina Shea writes,

> Christians in many parts of the world suffer brutal torture, arrest, imprisonment, and even death—their homes and communities laid waste—for no other reason than that they are Christians. The shocking, untold story of our time is that more Christians have died this century simply for being Christians than in the first nineteen centuries after the birth of Christ. They have been persecuted and martyred before an unknowing, indifferent world and a largely silent Christian community. And as their suffering intensifies, our silence becomes more stark.[48]

Shea speaks of our silence about their persecution and encourages Christians in this country to appeal to governmental powers so that this persecution may be eased. I believe her statement convicts us on another level as well. Cannot "our silence" refer to the fact that we simply are not witnessing? Why is it that we enjoy freedom of religious expression but refuse to take advantage of it? Why is it that many Christians in this world do not enjoy such freedoms, yet they risk life and property in order to share with others the good news of Jesus?

It is the epitome of arrogance to believe that we, American Christians, should be free to witness without an attached stigma of fanaticism. For many, it is the fear of being labeled a fanatic that keeps them from witnessing. How dare we think, if we should stand publicly for Christ, that the world ought to applaud and congratulate us! Following Jesus has always been a fanatical thing to do. A fanatic may be defined as a religious zealot. When Jesus cleared the Temple of money changers early in His ministry, His disciples quoted Psalm 69:9, "zeal for your house has consumed me" (see also John 2:17). Jesus' actions that day were fanatical. In fact, there is little He did that could not bear that designation. Ironically, we claim to be followers of a fanatic, yet want nothing of His fanaticism. We want all the blessings of association with Jesus, but none of the hostility He said we would encounter if we were faithful to Him. We have opted for the easy path.

Why has God seemingly granted American Christians a moment in time that is relatively persecution-free? Freedom of speech, freedom to congregate, and freedom to worship have given us an open door to evangelize our nation. Indeed, with these freedoms we became the greatest missionary-sending force in the world. At the same time, the lost population of America has mushroomed to the point that our beloved country is, by population, the third largest lost nation in the world. Only China and India have a greater population of lost people. Our sacred freedoms have made us soft. We have taken for granted this wonderful freedom to speak for Jesus without threat of retaliation. Being free to speak we have nonetheless chosen to remain silent.

No such religious freedoms exist in China, but there, under constant threat of imprisonment or death, the voice of witness rings clearly. Consequently, the church, mostly underground cells or home churches, thrives and grows as the flames of persecution fan evangelistic passion. Shea writes, "In China today there are more Christians in prison because of religious activities than in any other nation in the world."[49]

I have never known any real fear of persecution. How do I explain, then, the fact that my palms get sweaty, my throat becomes dry, my lips parched, and my pulse rate soars when I attempt to witness to someone? We have allowed an irrational fear of rejection to keep us from speaking Jesus to the lost people around us. Thom Rainer has found that many lost people are very receptive to the gospel if only someone would share it with them. His research reveals that "82 percent of the unchurched are at least 'somewhat likely' to attend church if they are invited . . . . More than eight out of ten of the unchurched said they would come to church if they were invited."[50] The question then is why are Christians not inviting their lost friends and neighbors to church? Rainer found that "only 21 percent of active churchgoers invite *anyone* to church in the course of a year. But only 2 percent of church members invite an unchurched person to church."[51] Rainer calls this problem "evangelistic apathy."[52] Another surprising fact that Rainer discovered is that "very few of the unchurched have had someone share with them how to become a Christian."[53] On a purely statistical level, Rainer concludes that "over 17 million people will accept Christ if presented with the gospel. Another 43 million are close . . . The vast majority of the receptive unchurched people in America told us that no one had ever invited them to church or shared the gospel with them."[54]

Of course, inviting people to church is a beginning, but the crucial issue is whether we will explain the gospel to them. Alvin Reid relates a story of a woman who, after her conversion, said to the woman who finally got up the courage to witness to her, "You have invited me to church. You have invited me to Sunday School . . . But you have never told me about Jesus. Why?"[55] Might not our friends, neighbors, work associates, and family members ask us the same thing? Why have you never told me about Jesus? Can we answer that question with anything other than the truth? We are ashamed of the gospel! Paul was on the other side of the issue, claiming, "I am not ashamed of the gospel, for it is the power of God for salvation to everyone who believes" (Romans 1:16). Paul encouraged young Timothy with these words: "Do not be ashamed of the testimony of our Lord . . . but join with me in suffering for the gospel according to the power of God" (2 Timothy 1:8).

All around the world the voice of the martyrs cries out to us, but we do not want to hear what they are saying. We are at ease in our private Zions. We have grown comfortable with our indifference and silence. With each new martyr, though, their voice grows louder and if we will listen we can hear their plea. This is the martyrs' cry—"Come die with us! Come die for Jesus!" How odd this invitation seems to those who are safe and secure. Our silence, both to the martyrs' plight and to a lost world, is our measured response—"No thanks. I rather enjoy my life. I think I will keep it." What we have missed, however, is that the martyrs' cry is also the cry of Jesus, for He, too, by these words said, "Come die with me":

If anyone wishes to come after Me, he must deny himself, and take up his cross daily and follow Me. For whoever wishes to save his life will lose it, but whoever loses his life for My sake, he is the one who will save it. For what is a man profited if he gains the whole world, and loses or forfeits himself? For whoever is ashamed of Me and My words, the Son of Man will be ashamed of him when He comes in His glory, and the glory of the Father and of the holy angels (Luke 9:23-26).

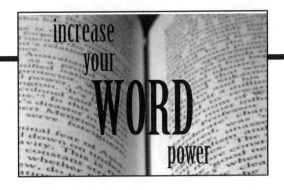

increase your WORD power

1   Read Revelation 2:4-5. Have you lost your first love? Do you remember the passion for Jesus that marked your life when you were first saved? How can you recapture that passion? Jesus indicates in verse 5 that repentance is the key. We need to repent of our lack of zeal for the Lord Jesus. Offer a prayer of repentance to the Lord.

2   Make a commitment to pray for Christians around the world who are facing tremendous persecution for their faith. Pray that God would grant them boldness to continue witnessing. Pray that God would make you bold in witness.

CHAPTER SEVENTEEN

UNTIL THE TRUMPET SOUNDS

Throughout the Bible trumpets were employed to send various messages to the people of God. Blasts on a trumpet were used to call the people to attention, to sound an alarm of approaching danger, to rally the troops, and even to initiate a time of rejoicing after a victory. It will be the sound of a trumpet that signals the end of the age and the coming of the Lord Jesus to gather His people to himself. In His Olivet Discourse Jesus said, "And then the sign of the Son of Man will appear in the sky, and then all the tribes of the earth will mourn, and they will see the Son of Man coming on the clouds of the sky with power and great glory. And He will send forth His angels with a great trumpet, and they will gather together His elect from the four winds, from one end of the sky to the other" (Matthew 24:30-31). Prior to this statement, Jesus had said, "this gospel of the kingdom shall be preached in the whole world as a testimony to all the nations, and then the end will come" (Matthew 24:14).

If you want to know when something is extremely important in Scripture, look for teachings that are doubly emphasized. Did you notice in this last verse that Jesus repeated himself? He said that the gospel would be preached "in the whole world" and that there would be a witness "to all the nations." It is no wonder that His last words to His followers just prior to His ascension were, "Go therefore and make disciples of all the nations, baptizing them in the name of the Father and the Son and the Holy Spirit" (Matthew 28:19). These final words conclude with a promise: "I am with you always, even to the end of the age" (Matthew 28:20).

The Great Commission, Jesus' marching orders for His church, delineates the scope of our witness. We are to go to all the nations and witness until the very end. In other words, we are always to be going and witnessing, making disciples as a result. There is to be no geographical limit beyond which we should not go. There is no time when we should call it quits. There just is no stopping point, except the return of Jesus. What does Jesus expect us to be doing until His return? There is no other answer but this: We are to communicate Jesus to a world lost in sin. Jesus exhorted His followers to be faithful to what He had commanded. He said, "Blessed is that slave whom his master finds so doing when he comes" (Matthew 24:46). Failure to be a faithful witness carries heavy consequences. Obedience and faithfulness will result in this spoken blessing: "Well done, good and faithful slave ... enter into the joy of your master" (Matthew 25:21).

Now, of course, it is impossible to be witnessing to some lost person one-hundred percent of the time. Should we fear that if we are not actually in the process of witnessing when Jesus returns that we will miss His blessing? By no means! What is emphasized in this parable is that we must be faithful in service to the Lord as part of our ongoing lifestyle. Our faithfulness in witness and ministry to others, bearing fruit for the Kingdom of God, is what Jesus has in view. And yet, multitudes of Christians have never attempted to intentionally witness to someone lost without Christ. Many Christians have never experienced the joy of leading another person to Jesus. Recognizing this huge void, Alvin Reid writes, "If we share Christ often enough, we will lead someone to Christ! The reason many Christians have never won anyone to Christ is because they have witnessed very little."[56]

So, I ask you, here at the end of this book, to think deeply about the consequences of leading a life that does not actively and purposefully communicate Jesus to others. First, I want you to consider the consequences for your own life. Are you willing to stand in God's presence without having been a witness? We are commanded in Scripture to bear fruit. Part of this fruit-bearing is the development of a Christlike, Spirit-filled life. Paul wrote, "But the fruit of the Spirit is love, joy, peace, patience, kindness, goodness, faithfulness, gentleness, self-control" (Galatians 5:22-23). The other aspect of fruitfulness is put in terms of producing fruit or leading others to faith in Jesus. Jesus spoke of this in John 15. There is a progression in Jesus' words from bearing no fruit, to bearing some fruit, to becoming more fruitful, to bearing much fruit, to bearing fruit that will last unto eternity. When Jesus spoke of witnessing and evangelizing, He spoke in terms of a harvest: "The harvest is plentiful, but the workers are few. Therefore beseech the Lord of the harvest to send out workers into His harvest" (Matthew 9:37-38). Again He said, "Do you not say, 'There are yet four months, and then comes the harvest'? Behold, I say to you, lift up your eyes and look on the fields, that they are white for harvest" (John 4:35).

Jesus' desire for His followers is that we bear much fruit in this spiritual and everlasting harvest. How sad it will be to stand before God without any fruit as evidence of our faithfulness. Paul changes the metaphor from harvest to construction: "Now if any man builds upon the foundation with gold, silver, precious stones, wood, hay, straw, each man's work will become evident; for the day will show it because it is to be revealed with fire, and the fire itself will test the quality of each man's work. If any man's work which he has built on it remains [returning to the harvest theme of John 15: 'if your fruit lasts'], he will receive a reward. If any man's work is burned up, he shall suffer loss ['every branch in me that does not bear fruit, he takes away'— John 15:2]; but he himself will be saved, yet so as through fire" (1 Corinthians 3:12-15). This teaching is important. Paul does not imply that failure to bear fruit results in the loss of one's salvation, for even though the "work is burned up" and one might "suffer loss," the person "shall be saved, yet so as through fire." Nevertheless, multitudes of Christians have comforted themselves with the thought that it really does not matter if they witness or not because in the end they will go to heaven. This is a very selfish and nearsighted approach to the Christian life. It is concerned only with one's own well-being. It betrays a complete lack of concern for the eternal plight of others.

The second consequence of failing to communicate Jesus is far greater than the loss of rewards in heaven, for it is, in fact, the loss of heaven itself—not for the witness but for those to whom the witness never speaks. Our failure to witness results in the eternal doom of those to whom we should have spoken. If nothing I have said thus far has motivated you to speak Jesus to those who are lost, then allow me to ask you to think about the hell to which they are headed.

Years ago, I was talking to a man about the Lord and his need for salvation. In the midst of the conversation, he shocked me with his response. He told me that he knew he was going to hell and that he would just take his chances there. On another occasion, a young man told me that his parents had died without Jesus and were certainly in hell and that he would just go to hell to be with them. O how urgent our message is! There are no chances in hell; there is no togetherness in hell. Hell is final and dark where separation and aloneness reign. To be utterly and finally cast away from God's eternal presence is absolutely the worst possible scenario. No relief, no release, no end, no hope! In the movie *Conspiracy Theory* with Mel Gibson and Julia Roberts, Gibson's character, Jerry, is recaptured by those who had brainwashed him to be a mercenary assassin. Jerry had been trying to break out from under the drug-induced, altered state of mind that had him trapped. As his captor was injecting him again to bring him back into submission, he asked Jerry a question that haunts me: "Have you ever been to a place where there is no hope, only patience?" Our silence condemns countless people to just such a place—no hope, only endurance.

During the time that I pastored a small mission in Denton, Texas, I met and witnessed to a man who was putting off a decision to follow Jesus. He was not antagonistic toward spiritual matters, but he was horribly indifferent. He was pleasant to talk with and he encouraged his children to attend Sunday School. I could not, however, convince him to come to church or to consider Christ's claim upon his life. One weeknight as I drove from seminary up Interstate 35 to Denton to make some visits, I prayed not just for this man but also for myself. I guess I needed some incentive to witness to this one whose heart was closed to his spiritual need. I remember asking God as I drove to allow him to begin to understand how real and how awful hell would be. I do not have a good explanation for my visit with him that evening except that God, in part, answered my prayer. The temperature in his family room where we sat felt to be well over one hundred degrees, even though it was a cool evening and no furnace had been lit. His family was seated comfortably across the room, but he and I sat in the midst of invisible flames, faces flushed, and sweat pouring out of our bodies. I believe it got his attention, for he began attending church services not long after that visit. That night had a profound affect upon me as well. I learned never to take someone's spiritual condition lightly. To live without Christ is to miss out on many blessings and joys; to die without Christ is hell.

Not long after this unique evening, I awoke from my sleep and remembered every detail of the dream that I shared with you in chapter 10. I will not relate it to you again, but I do want to mention two unforgettable truths that God taught me from this dream. The first is that because of the silence of Christians, some people never understand the gospel well enough to make a decision for Christ. Their sins committed against a holy God are enough to condemn them and God is just in his final judgment, "for the wages of sin is death" (Romans 6:23), and "all have sinned and fall short of the glory of God" (Romans 3:23). God convicted me of my accountability for the souls of those around me. My silence—your silence—may condemn some loved one to a hopeless hell. This is the "watchman's" duty of Ezekiel's prophecy:

> And the word of the LORD came to me, saying, "Son of man, speak to the sons of your people and say to them, 'If I bring a sword upon a land, and the people of the land take *one man* from among them and make him their watchman, and he sees the sword coming upon the land and blows on the trumpet and warns the people, then he who hears the sound of the trumpet and does not take warning, and a sword comes and takes him away, his blood will be on his own head. He heard the sound of the trumpet but did not take warning; his blood will be on himself. But had he taken warning, he would have delivered his life. But if the watchman sees the sword coming and does not blow the trumpet and the people are not warned, and a sword comes and takes *a person* from them, *he is taken away in his iniquity*; but his blood I will require from the watchman's hand.'" . . . "Say to them, 'As I live!' declares the Lord GOD, 'I take no pleasure in the death of the wicked, but

rather that the wicked turn from his way and live. Turn back, turn back from your evil ways! Why then will you die, O house of Israel?'" (Ezekiel 33:1-6, 11 italics added).

Notice the relationship between the *one man*—the watchman—and *a person* who is not warned by the watchman. I believe that God gives every one of us the responsibility for some person. In truth, I believe that we are responsible for many people—every person with whom we have contact. Now look at that phrase: *he is taken away in his iniquity.* Who is responsible for the doom of this one person? The person himself is responsible for he has sinned, but the responsibility lies also with the negligent watchman who knew the ruin that was coming and failed to sound the warning. God's heart in the matter is revealed in verse ten. God takes no pleasure in anyone dying without Jesus. He calls those of us who believe in and follow Jesus to serve as watchmen to the lost that they may see the wrath to come and turn from their sins in repentance. Will you not blow the trumpet of warning for your lost friends and neighbors? If you will not, then God will require their blood from your hand. I am not sure what that means or how that will be accomplished, but I do know that I do not want to be called to account for such a failure in my life.

The second truth that arose from that very vivid dream is this: people need help deciding for Jesus. Lost people left to themselves will vacillate and hesitate and waver. They will misunderstand the very serious consequences of sin. In the confusion of this world's conflicting spiritual teachings, they will be deceived and will choose the broad path of the world rather than the narrow way of Christ. God has chosen, however, to speak the gospel to them through us in order that we may help them choose Jesus.

Let me conclude with a parable-like story that I heard somewhere along the way: *After having spent a very busy and fatiguing day, the Thompson family went to bed early. Mr. Thompson and the children fell off to sleep quickly, but Mrs. Thompson lay awake, restless and anxious. In the front room of their home hung the family heirloom—a beautifully hand-crafted antique cuckoo clock. The children loved to watch the little bird stick out its head as it chirped its pleasant "cuckoo, cuckoo." But tonight the cuckoo-chirping bird was distracting. Mrs. Thompson heard the single "cuckoo" marking half past ten. She was still awake thirty minutes later and counted eleven "cuckoos." She tossed and turned, heard the single "cuckoo" at 11:30 p.m. and was pacing the floor as the majestic cuckoo sang out its twelve notes at midnight. She returned to bed after the single chirp marking 12:30 a.m. She hoped and prayed that she could finally get to sleep and that the sole "cuckoo" at one o'clock would not wake her up. But, alas, she was awake at five minutes 'til. So, she waited for the bird to chirp its sole 1:00 a.m. chirp. She thought briefly that she might choke the breath out of that little stuffed bird if it dared be so cheerful at one in the morning. But then something strange happened, in a low mournful chirp the little bird "cuckooed." He did not stop at one, though, but continued on—two, three—and on—nine, ten, eleven, twelve, **thirteen!***

The Shadow of Babel

What? Thirteen!? Impossible! Frightened, Mrs. Thompson turned to her husband, shook him frantically, and said, "Honey, wake up! It's later than it's ever been!

One day soon the trumpet will sound and eternal destinies will be set. Truly it is later than it has ever been. The lost around us are running out of time. We must sound forth the watchman's trumpet, speaking Jesus to a language-challenged world until that final trumpet sounds, calling us home.

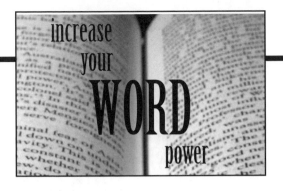

increase your WORD power

1 Revelation 3:20 says, "Behold, I stand at the door and knock; if anyone hears My voice and opens the door, I will come in to him and will dine with him, and he with Me." We usually relate this verse to unbelievers who need to open the door of their heart to Jesus. In reality, though, Jesus speaks this promise to believers who need to repent. Earlier in this letter to the church in Laodicea, Jesus had condemned the lukewarmness of the church members there (v. 15). Verse 20 is His hope that they would repent and open themselves to Him again. There is no area of our Christian lives where lukewarmness is more evident than in the area of witnessing. Enough of our apathy and excuses! Are you ready to commit yourself to being a consistent witness? Will you use your voice to speak Jesus to those around you? I pray that you will.

PERSONALIZE YOUR GOSPEL PRESENTATION

I was a seminary student still trying to overcome the crippling effects of my childhood shyness, attending the intense leaders' training for a new Southern Baptist evangelism tool, *Continuing Witness Training.* I had studied the material and had learned the outline but was fearful of the actual visits we were to make. I had joined dozens of other students and well-seasoned pastors at a church in the suburbs of Fort Worth, Texas. On the third evening of our training, I drove to the church with much fear and trembling, for we were to go out in teams and share our faith, using the outline we had learned. We made one stop, but nobody was home; a second visit yielded no opportunity to begin a spiritual conversation. The third visit went extremely well. The person listened intently, answering each question exactly like the material suggested. Our team leader seamlessly followed the outline and brought the person to the threshold of commitment to Christ, and then . . . he paused, smiled, and introduced us to a member of his Sunday School class that he had enlisted to role play the witnessing encounter. My head began to spin and my heart ached. I was a shy student needing to know that God would work powerfully in a witnessing situation. I felt betrayed and deceived. What I had just witnessed was not a witnessing situation at all (even though I had been praying for the person at the door as if he were lost), but a rehearsed "mock" witnessing encounter. I felt mocked. I had no new assurance that God would use me as I shared the gospel presentation that I had been learning. The one true attempt we made that night failed miserably. We were not able to get past the lead-in questions. At the end of the day, I felt set up and let down.

One shortcoming of many of the gospel presentations that believers are trained to use is that the words and phrases seem forced and fabricated. This is why the complaint of a "canned" approach is so often leveled against witnessing training programs.[57] Every person speaks in ways that are unique to his or her own personality. To force every person to talk in the same manner using the same words creates woodenness or stiffness in the presentation. The focus in such a witnessing situation becomes the struggle to remember exactly what one is supposed to say and to say it exactly the right way. While it is very helpful to employ witnessing guides and suggestions, it is detrimental to require total uniformity to a verbatim presentation of the gospel. "Success" in such witnessing encounters becomes not whether the lost person understands the gospel and takes steps toward faith in Jesus but on whether or not the presentation is done correctly. I am not asking pastors and church leaders to abandon evangelism training programs, but I am suggesting that Christians undertaking such studies be allowed the freedom to express the truths of the gospel with speech patterns that are appropriate to each person.

This is what the apostle Paul did. He so internalized the truths of the gospel that he referred to it as "my gospel" (see Romans 2:16; 16:25). From place to place, we find Paul sharing the good news in different ways and with different words. His guiding principle is found in these words: "I have become all things to all men so that by all possible means I might save some" (1 Corinthians 9:22 NIV). We must readily admit that every witnessing encounter presents a new set of challenges and our approach and our words must be appropriate to the age, gender, education level, and spiritual background of the one to whom we are speaking. Jesus addressed Nicodemus differently than He did the woman at the well (see John 3-4).

While we may use a different approach and vary our words from encounter to encounter, there are some basic truths that must be conveyed. I am in no way advocating a watering down of the gospel so that it is palatable to those who struggle with the exclusive claims of Jesus. If we change the truth statements of the gospel, then we are guilty of what Paul accused the Galatians of doing—that is, "turning to a different gospel—which is really no gospel at all" (Galatians 1:6-7 NIV).

So, we must protect both the essence of the gospel with its unchanging central truths and the privilege of explaining it with our own words and phrases. Part of the problem is that many Christians are not familiar with the gospel truths. They have difficulty in sharing those truths because they do not grasp the concepts themselves. The *Increase Your Word Power* sections after each chapter were provided to help you begin to internalize some of these timeless truths of the gospel. If you skipped past these sections as your read, you may want to return to them now and begin to think through some of the basics of the gospel.

Allow me, as a guide, to offer in outline form "my gospel." I have pulled together thoughts and ideas from many different witnessing tools and made them my own. I do not need to search for words when I share the gospel because I am so familiar with the concepts I am sharing. In what follows, I am not giving you statements that need to be memorized and then recited. I am presenting ideas that need to be internalized in your own thought processes. Once you have grasped the concepts, find your own words to express them.

There are four basic truths that the entire Bible conveys. Over and over again God states these truths and reaffirms their validity for all people in all cultures. As you share "your gospel", you need to include these overarching concepts:

• God has a loving plan and purpose for the one to whom you are speaking

•The prevalence and consequences of sin

•Jesus died on the cross to provide forgiveness for sins

•To be right with God, people must put their trust in Jesus

In simple outline form, these truths may take this form:

•God's love

•Man's sin

•Jesus' death

•Man's response

Digest these simple concepts. Make them yours and you will

never be without an outline of the gospel.

Now, let's flesh out these concepts a bit. Ask yourself what each truth means and what its significance is. For the first statement, I usually express the truth of God's love in terms of His plan and purpose for mankind. I might say it like this:

God loves you and has a plan for your life.

Second, the consequences of sin need to be addressed:

You have sinned and your sins separate you from God.

Then, the significance of Jesus' death on the cross:

Jesus died on the cross to bring you to God.

The fourth point is a little more complicated, for we must make sure the one to whom we are speaking understands what is involved in becoming a Christian. We will enlarge this concept in a moment, but for now we will summarize it with a statement like this:

You must respond to Jesus with faith and repentance.

You now have four statements that begin to explain the gospel. The next step is to add some Bible verses to "your gospel." Remember, the Bible says, "So faith comes from hearing, and hearing by the word of Christ" (Romans 10:17). The Holy Spirit uses the Word of God we share with people to draw them to the Savior. This is the very reason it is so important to memorize key verses of the Bible. Let's add some of these to our outline.

God loves you and has a plan for your life.
John 3:16 . . .
John 10:10 . . .

You have sinned and your sins separate you from God.
>Romans 3:23 . . .
>Romans 6:23 . . .

Jesus died on the cross to bring you to God.
>1 Peter 3:18 . . .
>Romans 5:8 . . .
>Ephesians 1:7 . . .

You must respond to Jesus with faith and repentance.
>Romans 10:9-10, 13 . . .
>Mark 1:15 . . .

By sharing your four main points and reading or quoting these Scripture verses, a lost person can understand God's claim upon his life and be drawn to Jesus for salvation.

We may now add another key ingredient—your testimony. According to the emphasis of your personal story, you can add parts of it to any or all of these gospel truths as illustrative material. Or, you can share your entire testimony at the beginning of your conversation and then move to your gospel presentation. Your story makes the gospel presentation personal.

There remains two aspects of presenting the gospel that tend to be the most difficult—getting started and calling for a commitment. We will leave the beginning for the end and turn our attention to the fourth point of your gospel presentation. Once a person understands that God loves her and has a purpose for her life, that she has sinned and is separated from God, and that Jesus died on the cross for her sins, she needs to understand clearly what it means to accept Christ as Savior and Lord. You need to be prepared to talk about repentance from sin, trusting Jesus alone for forgiveness, and surrendering control of one's life to Jesus. Once these concepts are discussed, you may invite the person to pray, inviting Jesus into her life. Once she does this, rejoice with her and encourage her to follow up her heart decision with baptism and church membership. You will want to think deeply about these concluding issues. A good way to do this is to review what the various evangelism training materials say about it. You may want to read through the gospel presentations of *Evangelism Explosion*, *Continuing Witness Training*, or *FAITH*.

I have always found that the hardest part of witnessing is getting started. How can we turn a conversation toward spiritual matters? I have found it helpful to allow the centrality of the Bible to be my lead-in. It is easy to ask someone, "Do you have a Bible?" or "Do you read the Bible very often?" Whatever his response, you can then say, "Can I briefly share with you the basic message of the Bible?" Most people will allow you to do so if you keep your promise to be brief. Be creative. It is easier to get started than we imagine. Take a deep breath, swallow hard, say a quick prayer, but by all means speak up and share the good news of Jesus.

REFERENCES

Barnette, J. N. *One to Eight*. Nashville: Sunday School Board, Southern Baptist Convention, 1954.

_____. *The Pull of the People*. Nashville: Broadman Press, 1953.

Bliss, Philip. "Almost Persuaded Now to Believe." *The Baptist Hymnal*. Nashville: Convention Press, 1956.

Bryant, C. E. "Two Win One." In M. E. Dodd, ed. *Two Win One*. Nashville: Southern Baptist Convention, n.d.

Coleman, Robert E. *The Master Plan of Evangelism*. Old Tappan, NJ: Spire Books, 1963.

Fish, Roy J. *Every Member Evangelism for Today*. New York: Harper & Row, 1976.

Hankey, Katherine. "I Love to Tell the Story." *The Baptist Hymnal*. Nashville: Convention Press, 1991.

Hesselgrave, David J. *Communicating Christ Cross-Culturally*. Grand Rapids: Zondervan Publishing House, 1991.

Hiebert, Paul G. *Anthropological Insights for Missionaries*. Grand Rapids: Baker Book House, 1985.

Kluckhorn, Clyde. *Mirror for Man*. New York: Whittlesey, 1949.

Leavell, Roland Q. *Helping Others to Become Christians.* Atlanta: Home Mission Board, Southern Baptist Convention, 1939.

Luzbetak, Louis J. *The Church and Cultures.* Techny, IL: Divine Word, 1963.

McLaren, Brian. *The Last Word and the Word after That.* San Francisco: Jossey-Bass, 2005.

Miller, Calvin. *Spirit, Word and Story.* Grand Rapids: Baker Books, 1996.

Nichol, H. Ernest. "We've a Story to Tell." *The Baptist Hymnal.* Nashville: Convention Press, 1991.

Rainer, Thom. *Surprising Insights from the Unchurched and Proven Ways to Reach Them.* Grand Rapids: Zondervan, 2001.

_____. *The Unchurched Next Door.* Grand Rapids: Zondervan, 2003.

Reid, Alvin. *Introduction to Evangelism.* Nashville: Broadman & Holman Publishers, 1998.

Robinson, Darrell W. *People Sharing Jesus.* Nashville: Thomas Nelson Publishers, 1995.

Shea, Nina. *In the Lion's Den.* Nashville: Broadman & Holman Publishers, 1997.

Smith, Gary V. *The Prophets as Preachers*. Nashville: Broadman & Holman Publishers, 1994.

Thompson, W. Oscar, Jr. *Concentric Circles of Concern*. Nashville: Broadman Press, 1981.

Wells, Marian. *The Wishing Star*. Bloomington, MN: Bethany House Publishing, 1985.

Yancey, Philip. *Soul Survivor*. New York: Doubleday, 2001.

Notes

1 All Scripture quotations are taken from the NASB (*The Holy Bible, New American Standard Bible*, The Lockman Foundation, 1995) unless otherwise noted.

2 Gary V. Smith, *The Prophets as Preachers* (Nashville: Broadman & Holman Publishers, 1994), 8.

3 Ibid., 7.

4 Alvin Reid, *Introduction to Evangelism* (Nashville: Broadman & Holman Publishers, 1998), 8.

5 Smith, 7.

6 Ibid.

7 Roy J. Fish, notes from a sermon preached at an Illinois Baptist State Association Evangelism Conference.

8 Roland Q. Leavell, *Helping Others to Become Christians* (Atlanta: Home Mission Board, Southern Baptist Convention, 1939), 54.

9 Brian McLaren, *The Last Word and the Word after That* (San Francisco: Jossey-Bass, 2005), 6.

10 Marian Wells, *The Wishing Star* (Bloomington, MN: Bethany House Publishing, 1985).

[11] Reid, 198.

[12] Ibid.

[13] Ibid., 185.

[14] Smith, 11.

[15] W. Oscar Thompson Jr., *Concentric Circles of Concern* (Nashville: Broadman Press, 1981), 124.

[16] Ibid., 130.

[17] Clyde Kluckhorn, *Mirror for Man* (New York: Whittlesey, 1949), 23.

[18] Louis J. Luzbetak, *The Church and Cultures* (Techny, IL: Divine Word, 1963), 60-61.

[19] David J. Hesselgrave, *Communicating Christ Cross-Culturally* (Grand Rapids: Zondervan Publishing House, 1991), 197.

[20] Paul G. Hiebert, *Anthropological Insights for Missionaries* (Grand Rapids: Baker Book House, 1985), 45.

[21] Hesselgrave, 199.

[22] Smith, 11.

[23] Hesselgrave, 132.

24 Ibid., 135.

25 Ibid., 143.

26 Ibid., 105.

27 Roy J. Fish, *Every Member Evangelism for Today* (New York: Harper & Row, 1976), vii.

28 Ibid., 1.

29 Ibid., 2.

30 If by "programmed evangelism" the authors mean a systematic approach to evangelism training, then I am in more agreement with them. A programmed approach to evangelism, however, seems to limit witnessing to the particular day of the week earmarked for the church's evangelism program.

31 H. Ernest Nichol, "We've a Story to Tell," *The Baptist Hymnal* (Nashville: Convention Press, 1991), 586.

32 Katherine Hankey, "I Love to Tell the Story," *The Baptist Hymnal* (Nashville: Convention Press, 1991), 572.

33 Philip Bliss, "Almost Persuaded Now to Believe," *The Baptist Hymnal* (Nashville: Convention Press, 1956), 248.

34 Calvin Miller, *Spirit, Word and Story* (Grand Rapids: Baker Books, 1996), 144.

35 Ibid., 151.

36 Ibid., 148.

37 Ibid., 155.

38 Robert E. Coleman, *The Master Plan of Evangelism* (Old Tappan, NJ: Spire Books, 1963), 38-49.

39 Philip Yancey, *Soul Survivor* (New York: Doubleday, 2001), 110.

40 Thom Rainer, *Surprising Insights from the Unchurched and Proven Ways to Reach Them* (Grand Rapids: Zondervan, 2001), 43.

41 Ibid., 35.

42 Ibid., 23.

43 C. E. Bryant, "Two Win One," in M. E. Dodd, ed., *Two Win One* (Nashville: Southern Baptist Convention, n.d.), 17.

44 J. N. Barnette, *The Pull of the People* (Nashville: Broadman Press, 1953).

45 J. N. Barnette, *One to Eight* (Nashville: Sunday School Board, Southern Baptist Convention, 1954), 1.

46 Reid, 11.

[47] Ibid.

[48] Nina Shea, *In the Lion's Den* (Nashville: Broadman & Holman Publishers, 1997), 1.

[49] Ibid., 58.

[50] Thom Rainer, *The Unchurched Next Door* (Grand Rapids: Zondervan, 2003), 24-25.

[51] Ibid., 25.

[52] Ibid.

[53] Ibid., 26.

[54] Ibid., 46-7.

[55] Reid, 9.

[56] Reid, 15.

[57] "Some people criticize memorized presentations because they are 'canned'. In my experience, *any* presentation of the gospel—a marked New Testament, tract, or testimony—is canned, if the person sharing Christ doesn't care about the person hearing the message. But the discipline such an approach offers has aided many believers in their growth in personal evangelism." Reid, 198.